William of Ockham and the Divine Freedom

by

Harry Klocker, S.J.

With Thanks

Harry Klocker, sj

Marquette University Press
Milwaukee Wisconsin 53233
1992

© 1992, Marquette University Press

Printed in the United States of America
ISBN   0-87462-001-5
Library of Congress Catalogue Number: 92-082567

Deo omnipotenti

in cujus voluntate est

pax nostra.

My sincere thanks to those who in one way or another have contributed to this small volume:

to Mrs. Savina Tonella for her flawless typing of the manuscript,
to Mrs. Debra Penna-Fredericks for her work with the index, and especially
to the Reverend Anthony Daly, S.J., for his critical reading of the manuscript.

Copyright Acknowledgements

Franciscan Studies, Vol. 45, Annual XXIII, 1985. "Ockham and the Divine Freedom."

The Illif Review, Winter, 1983. "Ockham: A Note on Knowledge and Certitude."

The Modern Schoolman, January, 1958. "Ockham and the Cognocibility of God."
_____March, 1966. "Ockham and Finality."
_____May, 1980. "Ockham and the Divine Ideas."

The Thomist, January, 1960. "Ockham and Efficient Causality."
_____July, 1980. "William of Ockham and the Self."

Table of Contents

Preface

Life

 illiam of Ockham was born in Ockham in Surrey somewhere around 1290 A.D. He entered the Franciscans and began the study of theology in 1310 at Oxford. From 1315 until 1319 he would have lectured on the Bible and on the *Sentences of Peter Lombard*. The next five years he was engaged in writing and disputation. Ockham completed all the studies for the doctorate but never actually taught as a Master—hence the title "Inceptor," or Beginner.

In 1323 John Lutterell, a former chancellor at Oxford, wrote to the pope at Avignon to complain about the orthodoxy of some fifty-six propositions taken from Ockham's commentary on the *Sentences*. Ockham was summoned to Avignon in 1324 to reply to Lutterell's charges. Despite the rather severe criticism of the commission the process was never brought to a formal conclusion.

Aware, perhaps, that the decision of the papal commission would be anything but favorable, Ockham fled from Avignon in 1328 along with Michael Cesena, the Master General of the Franciscans. They went first to Pisa and then on to Munich where they were taken under the protection of Ludwig of Bavaria. It was here that Ockham joined Ludwig in his struggle with the pope over the extent of papal power with regard to the secular state. He also opposed the pope in the fight over evangelical poverty as it was understood in the Franciscan order. It was in this same year, 1328, that Ockham was excommunicated. In

1347 he appealed to Rome for reconciliation. However, before any answer could be received, Ockham died in Munich in 1349.

Works

Ockham's collected works include the usual *Commentary on the Sentences of Peter Lombard*, of which the first book is considered to be an *Ordinatio*; that is, it was written by Ockham himself. The commentaries on the other three books are *Reportationes*; that is, they are taken from notes and comments on his lectures. They may or may not have been approved by the author himself. The following works are almost entirely philosophical and indicated clearly his Aristotelian background. They are the *Expositio in Librum Porphyrii*, the *Expositio In Librum Predicamentorum*, and the *Expositio in duos Libros Elenchorum*. There is also an *Expositio in Libros Perihermenias*. Ockham also wrote a commentary on the physics (natural philosophy) of Aristotle, the *Expositio super octo Libros Physicorum*. Added to these are a *Summa Totius Logicae*, *Summulae in Libros Physicorum*, and *Quaestiones in Libros Physicorum*. The *Tractatus de Successivis*, although compiled by someone else, is considered an authentic expression of Ockham's teaching.

Ockham's strictly theological works include the following: *Quodlibeta Septem*, *Tractatus de Sacramento Altaris*, and the *Tractatus de praedestinatione et de praescientia Dei et de futuris contingentibus*. The authenticity of the *Centiloquium Theologicum* remains doubtful, although it certainly contains Ockhamistic teaching.

As was mentioned above, in 1328 Ockham fled from Avignon and took refuge at the court of Ludwig of Bavaria. It was here that his political works were written which defended the temporal rights of the emperor against the papacy. He was also involved in the dispute with the pope over the problem with Franciscan poverty. During this period he composed the following works: the *Opus nonagenta dierum*, *Compendium errorum Joannis papae XXII*, *Octo quaestiones de potestate papae*, *An princeps pro suo succursu scilicet guerrae possit recipere bona ecclesi-*

arum etiam invito papa, Consultatio de causa matrimoniali, and the *Dialogus inter magistrum et discipulum de imperatorum et pontificum potestate.* It is important to note here that critical editions of Ockham's philosophical and theological works or sections of those works are being published by the Institute of Franciscan Studies at the University of St. Bonaventure in New York. A list of the works published to date can be found in the bibliography at the end of this book.

The Attack on Scotus and his Predecessors

It is not uncommon in the historians of later medieval philosophy to see Ockham depicted as the negative critic of earlier scholasticism and in particular Duns Scotus. That such criticism is there is evident enough. In Ockham's world of absolute singulars there could be nothing like the composition resulting from the formal intelligibilities of Scotistic realism. Scotus had proposed such *Formalitates* to insure an objective ground for the universal concepts produced by the intellect. Ockham saw only a latent Platonism here and restricted all such formal distinctions to the mind as it viewed the existing singular from various aspects. Whatever exists is singular, totally so, and any composition would result in a singular being composed of many singulars. Neither could there be any relations between such singulars seen as really distinct from the singular objects involved. Such relations would themselves be singulars, and there could be no end to such a process. It was another way for Ockham to dispense with any necessity in a created order and to insure that creation was totally dependent on both the absolute and ordinary power of God.

From such a starting point it is not difficult to see how Ockham was able to expand his critique to other areas as well. He saw all attempts to demonstrate the existence of God as only probable arguments at best. The doctrine of Divine Ideas, held by all of his predecessors back to St. Augustine, was radically changed to fit his own theory of cognition and creation. There is in all this an almost drastic reshaping of previous philosophical teaching, be it Platonic or Aristotelian.

The Condemned Propositions

In 1323 Ockham was summoned to Avignon to reply to John Lutterell's complaint about fifty-six propositions taken from the *Commentary on the Sentences.* The process was never brought to completion, perhaps because Ockham fled from Avignon in 1328, when he suspected the case might go against him. Although many of the propositions were judged to be dangerous, false, subversive of theology and philosophy, heretical, contradictory, etc., no condemnation or excommunication was imposed at this time.

The majority of the propositions are theological in content and are only indirectly connected with Ockham's philosophy. The complete list can be found in *Recherches de Théologie Ancienne et Médiévale,* vol. 7, pp. 353-380, J. Koch. What follows is a sample of propositions dealing only with Ockham's philosophy. (The translations are my own.)

> Article 2. That intuitive knowledge of a creature considered as such does not necessarily concern the creature's existence or non-existence, nor does it look toward existence rather than non-existence.
>
> Article 5. When predicating wisdom or existence of God, the predication is not about God Himself but only a certain concept (of God).
>
> Article 10. That intelligence and will which are predicated of God are not God; just as no attribute is the same as the Divine Essence.
>
> Article 30. That nothing is known or understood of any substance; science is only of concepts.
>
> Article 38. That there is no relation of reason of God to creatures.
>
> Article 41. That genus is not intrinsic to the thing of which it is the genus.
>
> Article 54. That a proposition such as "God is wisdom, goodness, life" is not intelligible.

It is clear that the propositions listed above and taken as they stand would cause more than a little consternation among those who identified themselves as followers of Aquinas or Duns Scotus. It is also not surprising that later historians of philosophy and text book writers would see in Ockham someone who critically attacked the great theological systems of the earlier days and substituted for them a logical nominalism and philosophical fideism.

Perhaps it is not that simple. There were also the condemnations of Latin Averroism in 1270 and again in 1277. Any theologian writing after that was well aware of what had been condemned. One of the Catholic doctrines which had been affirmed by the Roman commission was that which stated that God had freely created the world, and that it was not due to some form of necessary emanation. It was of supreme importance, then, to defend both philosophically and theologically the divine freedom and omnipotence. This book suggests that such was Ockham's primary concern. To accomplish it he thought it necessary to do away with any threat to that basic teaching. In doing so he may well have destroyed more than he saved. But the purpose was a noble one, and it would seem that the Venerable Inceptor was more than a mere critic of the past. Despite his obvious Aristotelianism there is much of a *"Fides quaerens intellectum."*

Introduction

A Traditional View

ne way to approach the philosophy of William of Ockham (1290-1347) is to begin with his epistemology and point out its limits and its inadequacy. From this perspective Ockham emerges as a severe critic of Duns Scotus and Henry of Ghent and to some extent an adversary of Aquinas. One can also find in him a critique of previous Augustinianism and the origin of a more modern way in fourteenth-century scholasticism. That *Via Moderna* for all its logical precision is judged as leading to a drastic restriction of philosophical truth and to a scepticism about any knowledge beyond the empirical order. As a result the whole area of faith is greatly expanded and becomes in turn the only safeguard against a scepticism introduced by philosophy.[1]

There are certainly adequate grounds in Ockham for such an approach. Against Scotus's world of formally complex realities Ockham consistently maintained a world of uniquely existing singulars, each of which was only itself and pointed only to itself. Knowledge of these singular beings was grounded in a sensible and intellectual intuition of their existential presence to the knower. All other knowledge became abstract knowledge which divorced itself from existence. Such abstract knowledge resulted in a relationship of concepts, a logic, a pattern of interpretations, which might be adequate as a possible explanation of the world

---

[1]Cf., for example, Gilson, E., *History of Christian Philosophy in the Middle Ages* (Random House, NY, 1955), p. 489.

but which could give no guarantee of its existential validity.
Such validity was always reserved for the initial intuition.

A prime example of this is Ockham's treatment of causality. He
certainly seems to have held that cause and effect were operative
in the world of singulars. But to attempt to establish causality
philosophically was quite another question. If all one can intuit
is the singular in itself with no distinct reference to any other,
then causality had to be reduced to a more or less constant
association of two singulars. This association always remained
a *de facto* one, and the assertion that such a situation could be
affirmed beyond experience remained probable at best. How
could one affirm a cause which had not been experienced in
conjunction with a given effect? He is equally reticent about
final causality. He saw no way to establish finality in nature.
Nature was only itself being itself and would act like itself
whether there was an ultimate final cause or not. Ockham was
willing to admit some sort of finality in intellectual beings, for
such beings do propose ends for themselves and act to accomplish them. But such ends also do not point beyond themselves
to any ultimate end such as beatitude. Because of the freedom of
the will he saw any end as rejectable including final beatitude.

Granted such a view of causality there is little hope in Ockham
for any proof of the existence of God based on the contingency
of the finite. He explicitly rejects any proofs from efficient or
final causality; nor does he have any use for an *a priori* proof, such
as Anselm's argument. Secondary causality, for all we know,
might well terminate at a creature to whom God had given the
power to create. It also might go back into a multiplicity of
causes, each of which is the cause of all the effects in a given
order.

Ockham certainly held by faith that the finite was produced by
the *fiat* of a creating God. But philosophy can provide only
persuasive reasons for such a conclusion. Furthermore, it was
also true that God could produce any and all effects attributed to
secondary causes. It is a least possible, then, that there is no
secondary causality operative at all. It is also possible that such
a creating God could take the place of any secondary cause in any

causal series. His position is well known that God could create the seeing of a star without the actual existence of the star. Both the star and the seeing are distinct entities, one of which does not necessarily demand the other.

It is true that Ockham seems to hold a proof of God's existence based on the conservation of an effect. But this, too, is not conclusive. In the first place he had explicitly denied the real distinction between essence and existence; and, hence, he could not argue from an existential factor in the contingent being to an existential source. In the second place, since he had found it impossible to rule out a creature as the source of the rest of finite being, there is no reason why the same creature could not be its conserving cause. The whole realm of the finite remained mute about any transcendent source.

It follows, too, that one can know very little, if anything, about the God whose existence is affirmed by faith. Ockham admitted that there was a proper concept of God. It was, however, a concept formed by combining various perfections found in creatures and denying the limitations found with such perfections on the creaturely level. One could, then, manufacture a complex concept taken from creatures but no longer applicable to any of them. Hence, it was a concept no longer proper to any creature and which could now "suppose," stand for the God Who remained unknowable in Himself. It was around such a concept that the rest of a philosophical theology could develop. But it would always remain a philosophy of a unique concept and valid only to the extent that conclusions which such a philosophy arrived at did not contradict the original intelligibility of the "God concept."

The foregoing is an admittedly brief and inadequate summary of Ockham's epistemological position and the conclusions to which it led him in metaphysics and natural theology. There is much more, as will be seen later, but the above provides sufficient ground for the position taken by those who regard Ockham as a philosophical sceptic for whom all certitude about a transcendent reality looked to the faith for support. Furthermore, to begin with his epistemology is not unwarranted, since Ockham began

that way himself with his discussion of the various kinds of
knowledge in the *Quaestio Prima Principalis Prologi* of his
commentary on the *Sentences*. It is not uncommon, then, to see
in Ockham a medieval Hume. There is, of course, a vast difference. Hume had no remedy for his scepticism. Ockham did.

A Different Approach

What I would like to suggest is that another approach to Ockham
may be just as, if not more, meaningful. This might be true,
particularly in the light of the historical situation in which
Ockham wrote. Aristotelian Averroism had been condemned at
the University of Paris in 1270 and again in 1277. Many of the
rejected propositions regarded the impossibility of a free creation or the necessary emanation of the first intelligence from
God and the multiplicity of the finite from secondary intelli-
gences.[2] Ockham was certainly aware of these condemnations,
and they must have been in his mind as he wrote. Hence, instead
of simply setting out to challenge all the certitudes of his
predecessors, his real intention may have been entirely different.
If Latin Averroism had challenged and denied the Divine freedom in creation and suggested that God could not act immediately
and in different ways in the finite world, then it was necessary
to defend the doctrine of the Divine freedom at all costs.[3]

Ockham then had to choose a starting point which would assure
him of establishing a perfectly free God. If in the process of doing
that he had to give up philosophical certitude in many areas, he
was quite willing to do so in lieu of another and quite different
goal. A free Christian God had to be preferred to either an

---

[2] For a listing of the condemned propositions, cf. Hyman, A. and Walsh, J.,
Philosophy in the Middle Ages (Hackett Publishing Co., Indianapolis, 1973), pp.
540 ff.

[3] Cf. Baudry, L., "Le Tractatus De Principiis Theologiae attribué à G. D'Occam,"
Etudes de Philosophie Médiévale (Paris: J. Vrin, 1936), pp. 42-43. Also Vignaux,
P., *Philosophy in the Middle Ages* (Meridian Books, NY, 1957), pp. 172 ff.

Aristotelian First Mover or some sort of Platonic Demi-Urge whose activity was predetermined by the eternal intelligibility of the Ideas.

There are two Ockhamistic positions which at least suggest the probability of such an interpretation. The first is his emphasis on the distinction between the *potentia Dei absoluta* and the *potentia Dei ordinata.* In the first question of his sixth *Quodlibet* Ockham expresses it well. The question is whether it is possible for anyone to be saved without charity.

> God is able to separate any absolute distinct entity from any other and conserve it in being without that other. But grace is a distinct absolute entity. Therefore.[4]

He then goes on to explain that God can do some things by His ordinary power and some by his absolute power. This does not imply two distinct powers in God. It simply means that for God to be able to do something is at times to be understood according to the laws ordained and instituted by God. This is called the *potentia ordinata.* But it can also be understood another way; that God can do anything which does not involve a contradiction, whether this is in accord with the ordinary laws established by God or not. This is called the *potentia absoluta.*[5]

---

[4]Ockham, *Quodl. VI,* q. 1: "Deus potest omne absolutum distinctum ab alio separare et in esse sine eo conservare; sed gratia et gloria sunt duo absoluta realiter distincta; igitur potest gloriam in anima conservare et gratiam adnihilare. Ergo" (OTh IX, 585).

[5]Ockham, *Quodl. VI,* q. 1: "Circa primum quod quaedam Deus potest facere de potentia ordinata, et aliqua de potentia absoluta. Haec distinctio non est sic intelligenda quod in Deo sint realiter duae potentiae quarum una sit ordinata et alia absoluta, quia unica potentia est in Deo ad extra quae omni modo est ipse Deus ...est sic intelligenda quod aliqua potest Deus ordinate facere, alia potest absolute, non ordinate, quia Deus nihil potest facere inordinate. Sed sic est intelligenda quod 'posse aliquid' quandoque accipitur secundum leges ordinatas et institutas a Deo, et illa Deus dicitur facere de potentia ordinata. Aliter accipitur 'posse' pro posse facere omne illud quod non includit contradictionem fieri, sive Deus ordinavit se hoc facturum sive non, quia multa potest Deus facere quae non vult facere....et illa dicitur Deus posse de potentia absoluta" (OTh IX, 585).

It is well to note here that this absolute power is restricted to the principle of non-contradiction. The Divine will may have an arbitrariness about it, but It is not capricious, nor can it will nonsense. The Divine Will is, after all, identical with the Divine Intellect. But it does mean that the Divine Will can act within the decreed order of creation in a way not consonant with that order. For example, in *Quodlibet VI*, question 6, Ockham clearly states that, where distinct realities are concerned, and especially where one is the cause of the other, God as the first cause of everything can do Himself what He ordinarily does through secondary causes. This, he cautions, does not happen in the ordinary course of events.

It is obvious here that Ockham is trying to safeguard the gratuitousness of both the order of grace and the order of nature.[6] If someone can be saved without grace by the absolute power of God, then surely grace remains a gift in the order decreed by God. And if creation itself depends on the free choice of God to give being, then it remains possible for God to operate within that order in accord with the rules He has laid down, or according to other rules—as long as there is no contradiction in His so acting. This admittedly opens up creation to the possibility of Divine activity which makes it very difficult to assert any constant or necessary order in that creation. At the same time Gilson's criticism of Ockham's position seems too harsh.

> At the top of the world (was) a God Whose absolute power knew no limits, not even those of a stable nature endowed with a necessity and an intelligibility of its own. Between His will and the countless individuals that co-exist in space or succeed each other and glide away in time, there was strictly nothing. Having expelled from the mind of God the intelligible world of Plato, Ockham was satisfied that no intelligibility could be found in any one of God's works.... How could there be a nature

---

[6]Cf. Oberman, H., *The Harvest of Medieval Theology* (Harvard University Press, Cambridge, 1963).

when each singular being, thing, or event, can claim no other justification than that of being one among the elect of an all-powerful God?[7]

Ockham's position seems to be more balanced than that, and, as has been mentioned, he never reduced God's absolute power to complete Divine arbitrariness.

It is obvious that in his attempt to thoroughly and clearly establish the divine freedom Ockham would have to make some radical changes in the philosophy he had inherited from his predecessors. These changes would have to be made in various areas and would have consequences in other areas as well. The whole metaphysical theory of efficient and final causality would have to be reworked. Augustine's doctrine of the divine ideas would have to be re-interpreted. Man's knowledge of God would come in for serious limitation.

It is our intent to follow Ockham as he proceeds in his attempt to establish the divine freedom. Some may think that he had to surrender too much on the level of philosophical knowledge; others, that he only succeeded in establishing a God subject to no meaningful norms in His activity. Whatever the outcome Ockham was certain that he had replaced a God Who was dangerously close to Plotinian and Avicennan necessity with a truly Christian God Whose free creation was now beyond question.

---

[7]Gilson, E., *The Unity of Philosophical Experience* (Charles Scribner's Sons, NY, 1937), p. 85.

I
Efficient Causality

t is in his treatment of efficient causality where it first becomes apparent that Ockham is trying to leave the created order open to God's free activity. His predecessors had argued for a necessary connection between effect and cause. Ockham did not deny that such might be the case where the *potentia ordinata* of God was concerned. But if one were to make such a necessary connection an absolute and universal one, then there was little room left for the *potentia absoluta* of God to function. Hence, if it were granted that God freely created the world, such a world of necessary relations would seriously limit the divine power to operate within it. A Christian God must be free not only to create but also to conserve freely what He had created and to act freely within that created order. Any connection between cause and effect had to be just as contingent as the things themselves. To maintain that contingency throughout creation Ockham had to revise the whole theory of causality so that it in no way threatened such contingency.

The next step, then, was to remove all necessity from the sequence going on in the created order and move it into the intentional order. A metaphysics of finite being had to give way to a logic of concepts. There are necessary relations between concepts, but there are none between things. Ockham's theory of causality makes it quite clear what happens to our knowledge of the metaphysical structure of reality, when the human intellect is restricted to an intuition of singular, sensible existents. St. Thomas had left no doubt about man's capacity to know the existing, sensible thing. He, however, had also made it quite clear that the mind could come to a certain knowledge of principles and relationships, which could not be directly intuited, but which were necessary for the existing sensible thing to be and to function the way it did. Thus he was able to assert the reality of such principles of being and operation. As a result, the universe of Aquinas is one composed, not only of things, but of real principles of things which necessarily co-exist to make the thing what it is and which explain, not only the whatness of the thing, but also the reason for its presence in the realm of limited existents. Such a universe can be validly approached from the viewpoint of philosophy and can be given a philosophically valid explanation.

Such, as will be made clear from what follows, is not the case with William of Ockham. Reality for him is no such composite structure. There are no realities which compose the real. There are just singulars, unique and uncomposed. The mind can and does abstract various aspects or formalities from these singulars, but such formalities cannot possibly be conceived as having any reality of their own outside of the abstracting intellect. For Ockham there is only one way to get at existence, and that is in an intuition of the sensibly existing singular. Any further intellectual activity prescinds from existence. Such an intellect can never again assert the extra-mental reality of any of its formulations or abstractions.

It is not surprising, then, that in examining the question of the possibility of proving the existence of God, Ockham had decisively rejected the validity of the ontological argument. If one could prove that God did exist, there was only one way to do it. That was to start with that world of experience which was the *primum cognitum* and from that world build an argument which would prove conclusively that such a world was unintelligible, unless there existed a God. It would seem that, if ever there was a man capable of arguing from the data of experience to the existence of a first cause of such data, that man was William of Ockham. With his theory of intuition of the singular existent, he had placed himself in direct contact with the existing world. He insisted on the contingency of that world and on its complete dependence on God. Did not that contingency demand necessity somewhere for its ultimate explanation? And was not causality a fact in that world of facts with which Ockham was concerned? And if the mind intuits the existing, contingent singular, does it not see in that contingent singular the evidence that marks it indelibly as an effect?

It is a bit startling, then, that Ockham not only answers in the negative but proceeds to attack the traditional arguments which had been used to prove the existence of God. It is impossible to understand that attack, unless one first understands Ockham's teaching on the nature of causality. In his treatment of causality Ockham willingly admits the Aristotelian division into four genera of causes. To each of these genera there corresponds its own proper type of causality. To be an efficient cause is to effect something or to act. The material cause gives being in a material sense. The formal cause communicates being formally to the composite. About the nature of the final cause he expresses some doubt, since he finds difficulty with the definition which is given: the causality of the final cause consists in moving the efficient cause to act. We shall restrict the present investigation to the nature of efficient causality.

In the *Summula in Libros Physicorum*[1] the efficient cause is divided and subdivided into various kinds. At the start, we may consider an efficient cause in the strict sense, in a wider sense, or in the widest possible sense. In the last sense the term *efficient cause* may be applied to anything which moves another thing, and it is called an efficient cause for no other reason than it is in some sense a mover. In the less wide sense an efficient cause is that which gives another thing a definite determination, as, for example, the builder does to the house he is building. In the strict sense an efficient cause is that which brings something new into

---

[1] Ockham, *Summula in Libros Physicorum,* pars 2, c. 3 (Venice, 1506). "Causa efficiens tripliciter accipitur: stricte, large et largissime. Dicitur stricte quando causat rem noviter existentem, ita quod nihil illius rei praecessit, sicut quando ignis causat ignem. Dicitur large quando est illa quae facit aliquid esse aliquale, et sic artifex est causa domus. Dicitur largissime causa efficiens pro omni movente, nec propter aliud dicitur efficiens nisi quod movet."

existence, as when fire produces fire. This last type of efficient cause can be subdivided into various kinds. There is the sufficient cause as opposed to the insufficient, the universal as opposed to the particular, the immediate as opposed to the mediate, and the first cause as opposed to secondary causes. The sufficient cause is identified with what is termed a total cause, and it is defined as "that which, when given all the proper conditions, is sufficient to produce its effect," or more exactly, perhaps, "a total cause is that which is sufficient to produce some effect and without which such an effect would not be produced."[2] Elsewhere the completely sufficient cause is described as that which produces the whole effect.[3] A universal cause is a cause which concurs with other causes in the production of their effects, while a particular cause produces just one effect, or at least only a few.[4] An immediate cause is one which, when placed, produces an effect and without which there can be no effect. God, we are told, is such a cause with regard to creatures.[5] Here in the immediate cause we find real and proper efficiency. It is the *causa efficiens in stricto sensu.*

---

[2]Ockham, *Quodl. I*, q. 1: "... causa totalis dupliciter describitur: uno modo dicitur causa totalis illud quo posito, omni alio circumscripto, potest effectus sufficienter produci; et isto modo, causa totalis dicitur causa sufficiens; alio modo dicitur causa totalis illud quod potest aliquem effectum sufficienter producere, et sine quo non potest talis effectus produci; et sic causa totalis et causa praecisa sunt idem. Primo modo loquendo, dico quod idem effectus numero potest simul habere duas causas totales, sicut idem calor numero potest simul produci a sole et ab igne, et a duobus ignibus.... Secundo modo, contradictio est quod idem effectus numero habeat duas causas totales...effectus habens duas causas totales primo modo, non dependet essentialiter ab altero" (OTh IX, 8).

[3]Ockham, *Scriptum in II Sent.*, q. 3-4: "...hoc est esse 'causa totalis' producere totum effectum... Deus concurrit cum causa secunda, licet posset producere effectum sine causa secunda, et per consequens potest esse causa totalis, tamen de facto non producit sine causa secunda" (OTh V, 63).

[4]Ockham, *Summula in Libros Physicorum*, 2, 3. "Causa universalis est illa quae cum diversis causis concurrit ad effectus illarum causarum."

[5]Ockham, *Scriptum in II Sent.*, q. 3-4: "... quia illa causa dicitur immediata qua posita potest poni effectus et qua non posita non potest poni. Sed Deus est huiusmodi respectu cuiuslibet creaturae" (OTh V, 60).

So far, then, we can say that according to Ockham an efficient cause in the strict sense of the word must be an immediate cause. It must here and now be responsible for the effect, and that effect must depend on it to the extent that without this cause there would be no effect. Such an efficient cause need not be the total cause of the effect, although it can be; and it will always be total in this sense that without it there will never be any effect. Such a cause is by its nature a sufficient cause, and it is universal or particular as the case may be.

There may also be and there frequently are many efficient causes at work in the production of an effect. They all may be necessary and immediate causes to the extent that, if any are absent, the effect would not be produced. Hence we can talk about primary and secondary causes. The primary, or first cause, however, is not necessarily unique and primary in all orders of causality. Here we have the first hint of a break in the causal line short of God; and, as we shall see later, it was a break which Ockham never managed to bridge. A cause is defined as primary or first in various senses. It can be a first cause according to primacy of perfection, as, for example, the sun is in relation to fire, when they both concur to produce an effect. Secondly, a cause can be called a first cause according to a primacy of non-limitation, as when one cause concurs in producing many effects. Thirdly, a cause may be a first cause with regard to a primacy of duration. This priority may be one of understanding, *natura prius*, or one of fact, *duratione prius*.[6]

Order between Causes

Between these first and secondary causes an order of some sort exists. At times this order is an accidental one; at other times it

---

[6]Ockham, *Scriptum in I Sent.*, q. 45: "...causa prima vel est prima primitate perfectionis, sicut si sol et ignis concurrant ad eundem effectum, sol erit causa prior primitate perfectionis. Vel est prima primitate illimitationis, ita scilicet quae concurrit vel concurrere potest ad plures effectus producendos.... Vel causa prima dicitur primitate durationis, et hoc potest esse dupliciter, vel quod praecedat secundum suam naturam, vel quod prius duratione causet" (OTh IV, 667).

is essential. The latter type of order is defined as that according to which the secondary cause depends on the first cause in its very act of causing. It also may mean that the secondary cause requires the first cause in order that the secondary cause may act as a cause. Lastly, it may mean that the secondary cause receives some power or influence from the first cause. Here it is interesting to note that Ockham seems to mean that this conferring of power by the first cause on the second cause may take place previously, so that the secondary cause may operate afterwards only by reason of this power conferred and not in strict conjunction with the first cause.

> ...God may cause some effect and afterward permit another secondary cause to conserve it and consequently to act, although this is not universally true; in fact, it rarely or never happens.[7]

This again seems to break the link between a series of ordered causes going back necessarily to a supreme first cause. Even if this never happens, the fact that it could happen is enough to throw some disturbing doubts upon any proof that attempts to demonstrate God as the first cause.

Nor does Ockham stop there but proceeds to question the analogical character of such essentially ordered causes. Scotus had stated that essentially ordered causes were specifically different and of diverse orders because one was superior to and more perfect than another. Ockham replied that *superior* can be taken to mean either a priority of perfection or a priority according to non-limitation. To take it in the first sense is to beg the question. It is to say that one cause is in a different order than another cause because the more perfect is the more perfect. The statement, therefore, must be taken in the second sense and

---

[7]Ockham, *Scriptum in I Sent.*, q. 45: "Secundo dico quod Deus est causa prima primitate perfectionis et primitate illimitationis et primitate durationis primo modo dicta.... Affirmativae patent, quia Deus est perfectior omnibus. Concurrit etiam ad omnem effectum, quod non facit quaecumque alia causa.... Negativa etiam patet, quia quamvis Deus possit primo causare aliquem effectum et postea permittere aliam causam secum conservare et per consequens agere, non tamen est hoc universaliter verum, immo raro vel numquam accidit" (OTh IV, 668).

must mean that every more universal cause is more perfect than a less universal cause. This, however, is simply not true. The more universal cause is sometimes more perfect and sometimes less perfect. A heavenly body, for example, which is not living, is less perfect than a living animal. But it concurs with an animal in producing another living animal. Here is obviously a case wherein a cause which belongs to a superior order is less perfect than its subordinate cause in an inferior order. Neither is it necessarily true that where essentially ordered causes are concerned, one can never act without the other. Animals are produced, not only in conjunction with a heavenly body and a particular agent, but also by putrefaction without the aid of a particular agent.[8]

Ockham's discussion of essentially ordered causes comes down to this: the essentiality of such an order seems to be a merely factual one. There is no intrinsic necessity demanding that all work in unison. In fact, at times the superior cause can and does skip an inferior cause in producing an effect which is in other circumstances connected with the inferior cause. Secondly, the superior cause is superior only in the sense that it is more universal; that is, it can reach to more effects. It is not superior in the sense that it has a higher order of perfection. Now in a series of causes where there is not necessarily a difference of perfection, where all may be of one order, or where the various orders may be mixed indiscriminately, there is no longer any reason for a necessary ordering of one to another. The only real connection seems to be that they must all exist, but it is not clear that even this existence must be simultaneous. Certainly it is clear that not all of these causes necessarily enter into the effect; hence, not all of them need be immediate causes. The distinction between essentially ordered causes and those only accidentally ordered fades away almost to nothing. This will become clearer, when we turn to a consideration of how Ockham comes to a knowledge of causality. In the meantime there is one more fact to be noted. Nowhere in his discussions of efficient causality does Ockham mention anything like a causal influx. Nowhere does he speak of the universal cause of the existence of things.

---

[8]Ockham, *Scriptum in I Sent.*, d. 2, q. 10 (OTh, 337).

There is no reference to a divine causality which has something strictly proper to it and which only such a cause can give to every effect. The effect is always one singular thing, and, while many causes may concur to produce that thing, there is no room in the thing itself to admit of various effects which can be traced to various causes.

To say that one cause gave existence, while another produced specification, would be meaningless to Ockham. Not only would it be to destroy the unity of the existing singular, but it would be an explicit denial of the previous identification he had made between the essence of a thing and its existence.[9]

Knowledge of Causality

That Ockham admits that there are causes actually operating in the real order seems evident enough. There has been some discussion about whether he admits causality as a universal metaphysical law. Manser thinks that it is undeniable that Ockham doubted the validity of causality in this sense, and he argues from Ockham's denial of the proposition: *Omne quod movetur ab alio movetur.*[10] Gilson seems to say that, while Ockham admitted the validity of the causal proposition, his understanding and explanation of what it signified are, in reality, a denial of the proposition.[11] Abbagnano states that Ockham's denial of the proposition, *Omne quod movetur ab alio movetur,* was a denial of a physical principle and does not necessarily include a denial of causality itself.[12] Let us turn to Ockham

---

[9]Cf. Ockham, *Quodl. II,* q. 7: "Unde idem omnino significatur et consignificatur per unum et per reliquum" (OTh IX, 143).

[10]Manser, G. "Drei Zweifler am Kausalprinzip," *Jahrbuch für Philosophie und Spec. Theologie,* 1912.

[11]Gilson, E., *Unity of Philosophical Experience* (Charles Scribner's Sons, New York, 1946), pp. 87 seq.

himself and learn, if we can, how a cause is known and what validity the causal proposition possesses.

We can begin by recalling two principles of which Ockham was very fond, and of which he makes constant use in his discussions, not only of cognition, but also of causality. The first principle is that only intuitive knowledge brings the mind into contact with the real order of things. It is in this way that the mind grasps the singular existent and grasps it in its singularity. All other knowledge is necessarily abstract. The second principle is that this real order consists of concrete singular things and of them only. These things, furthermore, are absolutely distinct from one another and are known as such. If there are actually causes at work, and if causality is something real, these will be known only in the mind's intuitions of existing objects. In these intuitions of the real order, what the mind apprehends is either a conjunction of two things or a succession of one thing after another. We know fire. We see that, when fire is brought into contact with wood, the wood gets hot. Take the fire away and the wood cools off again. Because in our experience this is always so, we say that fire is the cause of heat.

We have seen that for Ockham the real and proper efficient cause was an immediate cause. He had defined such a cause as one at the presence of which an effect was produced, and at the absence of which no effect was produced. That he is defining a proper cause in terms of being present, he makes quite clear.

> Properly speaking any cause is called a real cause at whose presence the effect is produced. From this it follows that a remote cause is not really a cause because its presence is not

---

[12]Abbagnano, N., *Guglielmo di Occam* (Lanciano, 1931).

enough to produce an effect. Otherwise Adam could be called the cause of me. But that is false because non-being cannot be called the cause of being.[13]

What he means is that not only must cause and effect exist simultaneously, but that they must also be experienced simultaneously. But is even this simultaneous experience of what he calls cause and effect enough to guarantee that the one thing is really the cause of the other? The answer is No. When I say, for example, that God is an immediate and principal cause, I can mean one of three things: first, that God could produce all effects without the aid of any creature; secondly, that when God co-operates with a creature, He does so only because He does not wish to produce the whole effect Himself; thirdly, the creature could not produce any effect, unless it were helped by God.[14] Accordingly, it cannot be demonstrated that any effect is produced by a secondary cause. Although in my experience it always happens that, when fire is brought near to something inflammable, that inflammable thing always burns, it could still be true that fire is not the cause of that combustion. God could so have arranged things that He Himself would cause the burning, when fire was brought near to something burnable.[15] All that the cognitive intuition gives me is the same sequence of events, when two things are brought into proximity with one another. There is no intuition of a causal influx. Hence, I can

---

[13]Ockham, *Scriptum in II Sent.*, q. 3-4: "Unde, proprie loquendo, quaelibet causa proprie dicta ad cuius praesentiam potest poni effectus et ipsa non-praesente non potest poni, potest dici causa immediata. Et ex hoc sequitur quod causa remota non est causa, quia ad eius praesentiam non sequitur effectus. Aliter Adam posset dici causa mei; quod non est verum quia non-ens non potest dici causa entis. Et similiter causa et effectus, proprie loquendo, simul sunt et non sunt.... Et sic si Deus concurrit cum causa secunda, utraque est immediata" (OTh V, 61).

[14]Cf. following note.

[15]Ockham, *Scriptum in II Sent.*, q. 3-4: "Et ex hoc sequitur quod non potest demonstrari quod aliquis effectus producitur a causa secunda: quia licet semper ad approximationem ignis combustibili sequatur combustio, cum hoc tamen potest stare quod ignis non sit eius causa. Quia Deus potuit ordinasse quod semper ad praesentiam ignis passo approximato ipse solus causaret combustionem" (OTh V, 72).

never assert with certitude that the one thing is the cause of the other.

In all this Ockham seems to be admitting that there is such a thing as causality, but that it is impossible to know concretely in what particular things causality is verified. Add to this the fact that the things which I experience, I experience as distinct one from another. The apprehension of one such object contains in itself no knowledge of another object. However perfectly I may know one thing, that knowledge will never lead me to the knowledge of another thing distinct from it. Even if it were granted that one particular thing did cause another, it still is not necessary to say that the knowledge of the one must cause in me the knowledge of the other.[16] As a matter of fact, it can never be known with certainty that one thing is the cause of another. As we have seen, the real and only cause may be God. Not only can God do whatever any existing object can, but there is also the possibility that in created nature an effect can be produced by another and unknown cause.[17]

To the objection that once an effect is known, we can know the cause from which such an effect naturally depends, Ockham answers that we can only know that in general there is a cause and that that cause must have some proper characteristics. What that cause is in particular, however, we can never know.[18] From

---

[16]Ockham, *In Prolog. Sent.*, q. 9: "... non obstante quod entitas unius esset causa entitatis alterius, non tamen oporteret quod notitia esset causa notitiae" (OTh I, 253).

[17]Ockham, *Scriptum in II Sent.*, q. 5: "Unde per nullum effectum potest probari quod aliquis sit homo, maxime per nullum effectum qui apparet in nobis, quia omnia quae videmus in homine potest angelus incorporatus facere.... Ideo non est mirabile si non possit demonstrari quod aliquid sit causa" (OTh V, 73).

[18]Ockham, *Scriptum in I Sent.*, d. 1, q. 4: "... quocumque causato cognito potest cognosci quaelibet causa in universali, puta quod habet finem et efficientem, et multae condiciones illarum causarum possunt ex illa re cognosci; sed illud quod est causa non potest ex quocumque causato in particulari cognosci vel cognitione propria sive aequivalenti" (OTh I, 436).

the existence and the beauty of a painting, we can argue to the existence and the ability of a painter. But we can never know directly the particular painter who did the work. The correspondence which is required between knowledge and its object to have objective validity is of an entirely different nature from that which exists between an effect and its cause.[19]

Nor is the similarity which exists between cause and effect enough to lead to a knowledge of the cause. The similarity will be meaningless, unless we already know that thing or person whose similitude is expressed in the effect. If one should see a statue of Hercules and had never before known Hercules, he would still know no more about Hercules than about Achilles.[20] It does not seem to have occurred to Ockham that from a statue of Hercules one could, perhaps, learn something about the sculptor. Practically the same answer is given to the objection that, at least if the cause is known as cause, then the effect proper to such a cause will also be known. To know a cause as cause according to Ockham already presupposes that I know the effect.[21] The argument here has been turned around, but he is still insisting on the same thing. From an existing effect I cannot know the particular cause. Neither from a knowledge of a given cause can I know that it must have this or that particular effect. Cause and effect are distinct things and always remain distinct. The knowledge of one never includes the knowledge of the other, just as the existence of one never includes the existence of the other.

---

[19]Giacon, C., S.J., *Gulielmo di Occam* (Milano, Società Editrice, Vita e Pensiero, 1941, T. 1, p. 432. "Dall'esistenza e dalla hellezza di una pittura possiamo argomentare all'esistenza e l'abilità di un pittore; ma la pittura non fa conoscere direttamente il determinato pittore che l'ha esequita. La correspondenza, che é richiesta tra cognizione e oggetto per avere cognizione oggetiva, é di tutt'altra natura da quella esistente tra effetto e causa. La causa puo restare un ignoto 'Noumenon di tipo Kantiano'."

[20]Ockham, *Prolog. in Sent.*, q. 9: "...quando notitia similitudinis causat notitiam illius cuius est similitudo, illa non est causa sufficiens cum intellectu, sed necessario requiritur notitia habitualis illius cuius est similitudo" (OTh I, 254).

[21]*Ibid.*

In attempting to evaluate Ockham's position on causality two points seem to be fairly clear. The first is that he seems to have held the existence of causality. Not only does he affirm frequently that there are such things as cause and effect, but he actually attributes universal causality to God. He speaks of the heavenly bodies as causes, and he thinks that, in many cases at least, we can safely conclude to the fact that created things exercise causality upon one another. It is true that he questions whether such statements can be demonstrated in the philosophical sense, but we are not at present concerned with that. In view of what Ockham himself says it would be difficult to deny that he admitted the validity of causality.

In the second place, it is equally clear that his analysis of how we come to a knowledge of causality leaves something to be desired. By the time he has finished that analysis there is little left to causality except a mere sequence of events. Because of his theory of cognition Ockham had to restrict knowledge of cause and effect to what could actually be experienced in the real order. Since the things which could be experienced were absolutely distinct and were apprehended as such, he was forced to admit that causality could mean no more than the constant succession of one thing after another. To admit an intuition of a causal influx distinct from A and B by which A could be called the cause of B would have involved him in great difficulty. To have an intuition of something meant that the particular thing in question existed in its own right as a distinct singular. It could then be known in its own right distinct from everything else. It could even be created by God and maintained in existence as distinct from everything else. Obviously there was no hint in our experience of any such thing. There was nothing left for him to do but to deny that the causal relation was really distinct from the thing itself.

Reduction of Causality to a Contingent Predicable

In answer to the objection that what comes to a thing accidentally must be really distinct from that thing, Ockham replied that an accident can sometimes mean only a contingent predicable. Causality is this sort of an accident, and as such does not signify anything really distinct from the thing itself. If *accident* is to be taken here as something really inhering in a subject, then causality cannot be called an accident.[22] Besides, to make causality something real in its own right would involve a contradiction. He argues from one of his favorite principles viz., that God can do anything by Himself which He ordinarily does through the medium of secondary causes. Now God can through the medium of secondary causes bring it about that a certain thing becomes an agent, and then there will come to that agent the relation of efficiency. God, therefore could bestow upon that same thing the relation of efficiency without the help of any other created cause. Now consider what has happened. We have something which God has made an efficient cause. But the only thing it can possibly have effected is that relation of efficiency. However, we have already said that God had done that. Hence, either we have an efficient cause that has effected nothing, or God cannot really do everything that secondary causes can do. In either case we end up with a contradiction.[23]

Similarly in the following question of the *Quodlibeta*, Ockham proceeds to reduce all relations to identity with some absolute. Aristotle, he tells us, did not really mean to say that relations exist outside the mind. In the predicaments the Philosopher is treating of the terms of propositions. Some of those terms are

---

[22]Ockham, *Quodl. VI*, q. 12: "...illud quod accidentaliter convenit alicui non est idem cum eo; sed respectus efficientiae est huiusmodi...dico quod 'accidens,' sicut prius patet, aliquando accipitur pro praedicabili contingenter; et sic relatio causalitatis est accidens, sed tale accidens non significat aliquam rem distinctam a rebus absolutis. Aliquando accipitur pro accidente inhaerente substantiae extra animam; et sic non est accidens ista relatio" (OTh IX, 629, ff.).

[23]Ockham, *Quod. VI*, q. 12: "...omnem rem quam potest Deus facere mediante causa secunda efficiente, potest per se facere sine omni causa secunda efficiente. Si igitur in isto efficiente ponatur unus respectus efficientiae causatus a Deo mediante isto efficiente, igitur potest Deus illum respectum facere sine causa secunda. Ponatur igitur in esse, et tunc sequitur impossibile: quia si Deus efficit illum respectum in ipso efficiente, igitur istud est efficiens... et non est efficiens nisi illius respectus; igitur non solus Deus efficit istum respectum. Et ita ex illa positione sequitur contradictio" (OTh IX, 632).

absolute, as those employed to signify substance and quality. Some terms are connotative, as those used to signify quantity, and some are relative. These signify a relation because they are coined to signify one thing and to consignify another without whose existence such terms could not be verified.[24]

Causality as such is a term of this kind. When we say a thing is a cause, we mean to signify the thing directly and to consignify another thing which we call an effect. The converse is also true. He is insisting again that what is apprehended is first one thing and then another. Because they are apprehended habitually in association with each other, or as following one upon the other, we can call one a cause and the other an effect. Neither cause nor effect signifies anything in the real order distinct from the things themselves. Cause and effect are contingent predicables which have meaning only in the mind.

It can be admitted, I think, that Ockham's analysis of causality was taken from the physical order. In that sense it was, as F. Copleston points out, a completely empirical investigation.[25] We can admit, too, that in this order it is often impossible to tell just what is the particular and immediate cause of a given effect. We do experience many effects the causes of which are hidden from us. But when we say, even if we do not know the particular cause of the effect, there is a cause, then we are going beyond the mere physical order and asserting a conclusion that is valid in all orders of being. This conclusion is based on and follows from

---

[24]Ockham, *Quodl. VI*, p. 16: "Philosophus in *Praedicamentis* principaliter tractat de terminis propositionum. Et isti termini, aliqui sunt absoluti, sicut termini in genere substantiae et qualitatis; aliqui sunt connotativi, sicut termini in genere quantitatis; et aliqui relativi, sicut termini in genere relationis, qui ideo significant ad aliquid et sunt ad aliquid, quia sunt instituti ad significandum unum, aliquid aliud consignificando, sine cuius existentia et cognitione non potest talis terminus de aliquo verificari.... Et ideo isti termini proprie sunt ad aliquid. Et condividuntur contra illos terminos qui absolute significant substantiam et qualitatem, et tamen isti termini aliter significant substantiam et qualitatem, et nihil aliud significant" (OTh IX, 643).

[25]Copleston, F., S.J. *A History of Philosophy,* vol. III, p. 72 (Westminster, MD Newman Press, 1955).

fundamental principles, such as: From nonbeing cannot come being; whatever is moved is moved by something else; potency can be reduced to act only by something already in act. We are saying, further, that in our experience of one thing acting on another we come to a knowledge that there is more here than just the association—however constant and habitual it may be—of those two things. In other words, we are affirming as something real a causal connection which makes understandable the constant association we actually experience. It is because of this that we can assert that the same reality must be at work in other orders where change and becoming also take place.

Ockham, however, made no such claim. His apprehension of change and becoming was limited to the world of empirical knowledge, and in that experience he admits nothing beyond the physical. In all of his analysis causality means nothing more than association, sequence, and succession. He knows only the things themselves which are associated, or which succeed one another with habitual regularity. Again it is his theory of knowledge which forbids him to go any further. All abstractive cognition presupposes an intuition of the singular existent. Such abstract knowledge differs from the intuitive in that it tells us nothing about the existence or non-existence of things. Furthermore, this abstract knowledge cannot go beyond the data of intuitive knowledge, but can only combine, relate, and draw conclusions. Now if the data acquired from intuitive knowledge, from experience of the existing world, give only association and sequence as far as causality is concerned, then how are we justified in asserting that causality is something real which transcends mere association in its metaphysical implications? And if some of those metaphysical implications are actually denied, as they were by Ockham, can we say that he meant any more by causality than the actual experience which he describes?

Conceivably it could be answered that, while all that is actually apprehended in experience is association and succession, it is still possible to justify causality metaphysically by reasoning on the data of experience. Yet such an answer would have its difficulties for Ockham. For him to admit this would also entail admitting that there was something in reality which was not and could not be intuited. In itself this is not an insurmountable difficulty, since Ockham is willing to admit as much of God or an angel. What seems to make such an explanation impossible is the fact that to admit it is to admit also that a causal influx, since it is real, is a singular existent in its own right. As such it would be absolutely distinct from every other thing. We have seen, however, that Ockham denied the reality of such relations as distinct from the things which are related. He made of them mere contingent predicables existing as such only in the mind. In the light of this it is very difficult to see how causality could have meant any more for Ockham than did the experiential fact. Gilson's conclusion seems to be entirely valid.

> Since the origin of causality cannot be found in the thing itself, or in the intuition of the thing by the intellect, it must be explained by some reason; and there is but one: it is what Ockham called *habitualis notitia,* and what Hume will simply call habit.

> True enough there are such things as relations of causality, and there is an essential order of dependence between effects and their causes, for their regular succession never changes; but since there is nothing more in causality than the habitual association of ideas caused in us by repeated experience, there is nothing more than a regular sequence of events in physical causality.[26]

It is little wonder, then, that we find Ockham refusing to build an argument for the existence of God on the foundation of the universal validity of the causal proposition. In the light of what we have seen, it is difficult to understand just what Ockham means when he refers to God as a universal cause. Certainly, there is nothing in his experience which makes such an affirmation possible. This Ockham realized. Whatever affirmations he may make about the divine causality—and he makes many—he was never able to accept any of them as really demonstrative. He gives many reasons for his refusal to accept them. Almost all of

---

[26]Gilson, E., *op. cit.*, pp. 87 seq.

them will return later to keep modern philosophy, or at least much of it, locked within the limits of physical experience.

It is evident, too, I think, what a tremendous difference there is between the realism of a philosopher like Ockham and the realism of St. Thomas. In the long run Ockham can be certain of only one reality—the concrete, material singular which is present to the knower and grasped by him in a singular intuitive act of the mind. When all relationships are identified with the ontological reality of the singular existent, the result is a universe of such startling uniqueness and independent realities that very few conclusions can be drawn philosophically about their origins. The result for metaphysics is disastrous. It can no longer be—as it was for St. Thomas—the expression of an insight into the existential structure of the real. Metaphysics, as Ockham conceived it, can only represent the mental relationships which the mind itself establishes between its various conceptualizations of a myriad of concrete singulars. This is a science of concepts, a logic, which enables one to think consistently and coherently about reality, but which gives one no assurance that reality is in any way like the concepts which one forms of it.

It comes as no surprise, then, to find Ockham asserting that much of what was once considered philosophically demonstrable is really in the realm of faith. It simply became impossible for him to separate philosophy from revelation and theology and retain any certainty. As far as any truth which transcends experience is concerned, that truth can be substantiated only by a revelation or an infallible authority. Take away that revelation and that authority, and man is left with sensible experience and probability. In such a situation there can be only one possible approach to certainty—the method of investigation and verification employed by the natural sciences. Ockham would find himself much more at home in the philosophical milieu of today than he did in that of the fourteenth century.

St. Thomas had given philosophy its charter, asserting that intellect was made for being and capable of achieving an understanding of being in its own right. Experience was necessary, of course, but it was possible to transcend experience because the mind could understand what was demanded to make experience itself possible. In understanding what lay behind experience the intellect gained a valid insight into the metaphysical structure of reality. Ockham recalled that charter. Philosophy might be able to get at being, but it was only sensible being with which it could adequately deal. In the last analysis it became apparent that philosophy could no longer deal adequately even with that. be—as it was for St. Thomas—the expression of an insight into the existential structure of the real. Metaphysics, as Ockham conceived it, can only represent the mental relationships which the mind itself establishes between its various conceptualizations of a myriad of concrete singulars. This is a science of concepts, a logic, which enables one to think consistently and coherently about reality, but which gives one no assurance that reality is in any way like the concepts which one forms of it.

It comes as no surprise, then, to find Ockham asserting that much of what was once considered philosophically demonstrable is really in the realm of faith. It simply became impossible for him to separate philosophy from revelation and theology and retain any certainty. As far as any truth which transcends experience is concerned, that truth can be substantiated only by a revelation or an infallible authority. Take away that revelation and that authority, and man is left with sensible experience and probability. In such a situation there can be only one possible approach to certainty—the method of investigation and verification employed by the natural sciences. Ockham would find himself much more at home in the philosophical milieu of today than he did in that of the fourteenth century.

St. Thomas had given philosophy its charter, asserting that intellect was made for being and capable of achieving an understanding of being in its own right. Experience was necessary, of course, but it was possible to transcend experience because the mind could understand what was demanded to make experience itself possible. In understanding what lay behind experience the intellect gained a valid insight into the metaphysical structure of reality. Ockham recalled that charter. Philosophy might be able to get at being, but it was only sensible being with which it could adequately deal. In the last analysis it became apparent that philosophy could no longer deal adequately even with that.

II
Final Causality

nce Ockham had questioned the universal validity of any argument based on efficient causality, there was little hope that one based on finality would fare any better. In a totally contingent universe it is hardly possible that any existing created nature could be necessarily ordered to any end, finite or infinite. At least such a proposition could not be demonstrated. That there were ends or goals toward which natural things strive seemed probable enough. But that such ends were necessary objects to which nature was ordered went far beyond any real or possible experience. Even goals known and sought after by rational agents did not necessarily indicate an absolute goal which transcended the finite. As will become clear, Ockham saw no difficulty in an infinite series of finite goals which a free human will could successively pursue *ad infinitum*.

Ockham began his treatment of final causality by doubting whether it could ever be established. There are three parts to his consideration. The first part deals with what Ockham understood and meant by a final cause. Secondly, he discussed finality as it is manifested in the empirical order of things. In the third part he turned his attention to the finality of the human will.

The Meaning of Final Causality

In the *Summula in Libros Physicorum* Ockham defines a final cause as that out of love or desire for which an efficient cause operates.[1] This final causality can be understood in two ways, and one is more accurate and proper than the other. Properly speaking, an end is said to be something intended or desired or loved, and it is because of this that an agent begins to act. According to this definition, it would seem that finality in the proper sense is limited to those things that act through intellect and will. And that is exactly what Ockham means. The remarks made about final causality are to be understood about those things which act from reason and choice—*a proposito et sponte*—since it is clear that with regard to such there is some final cause. In regard to those things which do not act through cognition and volition there is doubt if one can speak of a final cause.[2] If we do speak of a final cause with regard to such things, we do so only improperly; and we look upon them as if their activity were directed and intended by an agent, even where it is not.[3]

In the *Commentary on the Sentences* Ockham makes a little more clear what he understands by final causality. When it is said that final causality means to move an efficient cause to act, this moving means only that the end itself is loved by the agent; in reality this is the same as saying that the agent loves the end, or that something happens, or that something is willed because the end is loved. In the next few sentences the *finem amari* and the *agens amare finem* are still more clearly identified. By that which has been described as "the end to be loved" or "the agent to love the end" nothing is really acquired by the end, nor is there any influx from the end. Hence it follows that any motion connected with the end is purely metaphorical. And if it is

---

[1] Confer also Ockham, *Scriptum in II Sent.*, q. 3 (OTh V, 50).

[2] "Praedicta de causa finali intelligenda sunt de agente a proposito et sponte, de quibus manifestum est quod agunt propter finem et quod est aliqua causa finalis eorum. De aliis autem quae non agunt per cognitionem et voluntatem, magis dubium est an agent propter finem et utrum in talibus sit ponenda causa finalis" (*ibid.*, 2, 6).

[3] "Alio modo dicitur causa finalis vel finis pro illo quod secundum cursum naturae, nisi impediatur, sequitur aliud vel operatio alterius, et eodem modo sequitur ac si esset praescitum vel desideratum ab agente et isto modo finis reperitur in inanimatis, etiam posito quod a nullo cognoscente regulantur vel moveantur" (*ibid.*).

objected that the love by which the agent is attracted to the end is from the end as from an object, that there is causality here and, therefore, that the end really does move the agent, the answer is that, if love in the agent is caused by the end as an object, this is due to efficient and not final causality.[4]

It is one and the same thing, of course, to distinguish finality from efficiency and to deny that the causal influx in each case is the same. If we speak of efficient causality as a *motio*, then it is true to say that there is no *motio* involved in final causality or that, when we use the term *motio* of final causality, we are speaking metaphorically. Yet Ockham meant much more than that. In the fourth Quodlibet he says again that the causality of the end is nothing else than to be loved and desired efficiently by an agent, so that what is so loved becomes an effect. As we have just seen in the passage from the *Sentences*, the *finem amari* and the *amare finem* seem to be identified, so that there remains no distinction between the final cause in act and its proper effect. Here the identification is again insisted upon. We are told that just as the causality exercised by matter is nothing else than to be informed and the causality of form is to inform, so the causality of the end is to be loved and desired efficiently, and without this love and desire there would be no effect.[5] What Ockham is saying is that just as there is no distinction between a material cause and its effect, or between a formal cause and its effect, so there is no distinction between a final cause and its own proper effect.

---

[4]Ockham, *II Sent.*, 3, G. (OTh V, 50). "Dicitur enim comuniter quod causatio ejus est movere efficiens ad agendum. Istud moveri non est realiter aliud nisi ipsum finem amari ab agente vel saltem ipsum amari vel aliquid propter ipsum et hoc non est aliquid realiter nisi agens amare ipsum finem vel aliquid fieri vel aliquid velle propter finem amatum. Per istud autem quod est sic finem amari, vel agens ipsum finem amare, vel aliquid aliud propter ipsum, nihil aliud realiter acquiritur ei, vel etiam est ab eo. Ex quo sequitur quod motio ista finis non est realis, sed motio metaphorica. Et si dicas quod amor quo agens amat finem est ab illo fine ut ab objecto et ille amor est aliquid causale, ergo finis movet realiter, dico quod si amor causatur a fine amato, sicut ab objecto, hoc non est sicut a causa finali sed efficiente."

[5]Ockham, *Scriptum in II Sent.*, cf. 3 (OTh V, 50).

And he goes further still. Not only is final causality the same as to be loved and desired, but it is the same as to be loved and desired efficiently. From this it follows—and the conclusion is Ockham's own—that the final and efficient causes are only rationally distinct; that is, only their definitions are distinct. It is true that he admits that sometimes the two are distinct; but from the example he gives, it seems clear that he is speaking here about the thing which is an end and the thing which is an agent. God, for example, is both an efficient and a final cause in contradistinction to other things which may be either efficient or final causes.[6] If we consider, however, the actual causality at work, so to speak, then for the end to be desired and for the agent to desire the end is the same thing; and there is only a rational distinction between the agent's desiring the end and the agent's desiring the end efficiently. What Ockham means by *motio metaphorica* is not that there is a real distinction between efficient and final causality but rather that final causality can be reduced to efficient causality and that the only difference between them is a difference of reason and definition. It is a denial that final causality is something real in its own right.

Finality in the Nonknowing Universe

If it is true that Ockham reduced final causality to efficient causality, then it should follow that the task of proving any sort of finality at work in the world would be just as difficult as that of proving efficiency. Many of those difficulties simply reappear as Ockham turns his attention to a consideration of finality in

---

[6]Ockham, *Quodl. IV*, q. 1: "...causalitas finis non est aliud nisi esse amatum et desideratum ab agente efficaciter, propter quod amatum fit effectus.Unde sicut causalitas materiae non est nisi informari forma, et causalitas formae non est nisi informare materiam, ita causalitas finis est amari et desiderari efficaciter, sine quo amore vel desiderio non fieret effectus. Ex isto patet quod causa finalis et efficiens distinguuntur, hoc est definitiones exprimentes quod nominis earum sunt diversae; quia definitio causae finalis est esse amatum et desideratum efficaciter ab agente, propter quod amatum fit effectus; definitio causae efficientis est esse illud ad cuius esse sive praesentiam sequitur aliud" (OTh IX, 293).

the nonknowing universe. There is no reason why it should be any easier to prove a final cause at work than an efficient cause, and Ockham was never really certain that there were efficient causes operating. When dealing with efficiency, however, his task was a bit more simple. He had defined efficient causality in terms of presence and habitual association and succession. Of this much his empirical intuitions of reality could assure him. But when it came to finality in that same empirical order, the whole situation became somewhat more complicated. Ockham had defined final causality most properly as that which is intended or desired and because of which an agent begins to operate. Hence essentially and in its strictest sense finality demands a knowing agent, one which is capable of apprehending an end and desiring it. This alone would create difficulties in explaining finality in things devoid of cognition. But not only had Ockham demanded cognition and desire in his agent, he had also set up freedom to choose ends as a necessary constituent of finality in the strict sense. *"Praedicta de causa finali intelligenda sunt a proposito et sponte."*[7] It is not surprising then that he could immediately write that there was "more doubt about whether things devoid of knowledge and volition really acted for an end."[8]

Understanding final cause in this strict sense. Ockham said that inanimate things, if they are not moved and directed by some agent, do not have an end.[9] In one sense the statement is true, and his meaning is quite clear. An arrow may be made for shooting; but unless someone directs it to the target, it will never achieve the purposes for which it was made. Even here we might distinguish between the end and the acquisition of the end, and argue that the failure of the latter does not deny the presence of

---

[7]Ockham, *Quodl. IV*, q. 1 (OTh IX, 293).

[8]*Ibid.*

[9]"Causa finalis dupliciter accipitur, uno modo propriissime, et sic finis dicitur aliquod intentum sive desideratum vel amatum propter quod agens agit. Sic naturalia pure inanimata, si non moveantur et dirigantur ab aliquo agente, non habent causam finalem vel finem" (*ibid.*).

the former. There is no need to do so, however. Ockham is merely drawing a distinction, it seems, between inanimate artifacts and those things which owe their origin to natural causes. In these latter is it possible to point to finality at work?

There is another sense, admitted Ockham, in which we can speak of a final cause. It may mean that which in the ordinary course of nature, unless there is an obstacle, follows another thing and does so in such a way as if it had been foreseen and intended by an agent. In this way the end is found in inanimate things, even where they are directed by no knowing agent.[10] At first glance one is tempted to say here that what Ockham meant is that every agent acts for an end and the presence of such finality in nonknowing agents means that some cognitive agent has determined each to its own proper end. It requires only a little investigation, however, to make clear that Ockham was by no means repeating the thesis of St. Thomas that every agent acts for an end. In the fourth *Quodlibet* he states that it is neither evident of itself nor from experience that any given effect has a final cause distinct from its efficient cause, nor can it be sufficiently proved that any given effect has any sort of final cause.[11] Nor can it be argued that at least God knows these things and their operations, and has in His wisdom ordered them to an end. Such an argument presupposes that God knows all things, and that presupposition itself cannot be proved. To prove that God knows something outside of Himself would mean that it could be proved that God is the immediate and adequate efficient

---

[10]"Alio modo dicitur causa finalis vel finis pro illo quod secundum cursum naturae, nisi impediatur, sequitur aliud vel operatio alterius, et eodem modo sequitur ac si esset praescitum vel desideratum ab agente, et isto modo finis reperitur in inanimatis, etiam posito quod a nullo cognoscente regulantur vel moveantur" (*ibid.*).

[11]Ockham, *Quodlibeta, IV*, 1 (OTh IX, 295). "Non potest probari ex per se notis nec per experientiam quod quilibet effectus habeat causam finalem distinctam ab efficiente, quia non potest probari sufficienter quod quilibet effectus habeat aliquam causam finalem."

cause of this something. And this is impossible to prove.[12]

And when we turn to consider these natural effects in themselves, it becomes still clearer that what Ockham meant by his
"finality in a sense" is much closer to a natural determination,
which needs nothing beyond itself to explain itself.

> I say that it cannot be proved that the ends from which natural
> causes operate are known or intended by some agent. This is
> true only in the case of those things which can be moved
> differently to one end or another and are not determined by
> their very natures to one certain effect. It is only because their
> ends are known and that they are directed thereto that they can
> be moved more toward one end than toward another.... Merely
> natural causes, on the other hand, because they are by their
> very natures determined to a certain effect, do not require
> foreknowledge in an agent. At least reason alone cannot
> conclude that such is required.[13]

When fire is brought close to wood, the wood becomes hot. And
this happens whether it is intended by a knowing agent or not.
And if we ask why the wood should get hot, then, rather than
cold, the answer is simply that such is the nature of fire.[14] This,

---

[12]Ockham, *Quodl. II*, q. 2: "...non potest sufficienter probari quod Deus intelligit
aliquid extra se vel vult aliquid extra se, quia nulla videtur necessitas ponendi quod
intelligat alia a se, cum non possit probari sufficienter quod Deus sit causa efficiens
alicuius"(OTh IX, 115).

[13]Ockham, *Quodl. II*, q. 2: "...dico quod non potest demonstrari quod omnia
propter quae agunt causae naturales, cognoscuntur vel diriguntur ab aliquo; quia
hoc solum verum est in his quae possunt diversimode moveri ad unum vel ad aliud
et non determinantur ex natura sua ad certum effectum, quod fines eorum
cognoscuntur et diriguntur, quia aliter non plus moverentur ad unum quam ad
aliud. Exemplum est de sagitta, quae ex se potest indifferenter dirigi superius et
inferius, ad ante vel retro; et ideo requirit praecognoscentem eius terminum et
dirigentem, aliter indifferenter ad omnem partem medii moveretur. Et ita est de
aliis consimilibus quae non sunt causae mere naturales. Sed causa mere naturalis
quae ex natura sua determinat sibi certum effectum et non alium, non requirit
praecognitorem nec directorem, saltem ratio naturalis non concludit quod requirat"
(OTh IX, 115).

as Abbagnano points out, is to identify finality with the nature itself.[15] It is to explain the intelligible by blind force. It is to deny that nature is ordered to any higher end.

God and Finality

In the fourth *Quodlibet* Ockham takes up the issue directly and asks whether it can be proved that God is the final cause of any effect. He begins his answer by distinguishing two kinds of ends. First of all, there is the end which is given or predetermined by something extrinsic to the being which acts. Ockham calls it the *finis praeamatus vel praedestinatus a voluntate.* Secondly, there is the end intended by the agent itself. This end is first with regard to the intention of the agent, although it is last in the order of execution. Such an end is always something or at least some operation produced by the agent. Ockham immediately rules out such an end in the present discussion. God could not possibly be an end in this second sense. He would no longer be more perfect or more powerful than that which is ordered to the end, just as no effect is more perfect or more powerful than the cause which produced it.[16]

But can God be an end in the sense first described? Can it be proved that natural agents are predetermined and ordered to God as to their last and final end? In view of what we have seen, the

---

[14]Ockham, *Quodl. II,* q. 2: "...ignis approximatus ligno calefacit eum, sive hoc intendatur a cognoscente sive non. Et si quaeras quare tunc plus calefacit quam frigefacit, respondeo quod natura sua talis est" (OTh IX, 1116).

[15]Abbagnano, N., *Guglielmo di Occam* (Lanciano, 1931), p. 192.

[16]Ockham, *Quodl. IV,* q. 2: "...finis est duplex: scilicet finis praeamatus et praestitutus a voluntate, puta cum aliquis operatur propter se amatum vel propter amicum amatum; alius est finis intentus ab agente, qui quamvis sit primum in intentione, est tamen ultimum in executione; et talis finis est semper terminus productus vel operatio producta. De isto secundo fine non est quaestio, quia non est dubium quin Deus non sit causa finalis cuiuscumque isto modo, quia tunc Deus esset posterior aliquo quod est ad finem, sicut effectus productus est posterior producente" (OTh IX, 301).

answer comes as no surprise. It cannot be sufficiently proved or demonstrated, nor can it be known through self-evident principles or from experience, that those things which act out of natural necessity do so because they are predetermined or ordered to an end. The reason is that such action is invariable; and unless the agent is in some way changed, the action follows always a uniform, unchanging pattern. And therefore it cannot be proved that such an agent acts for an end.[17] Further on in the same article the answer is again insisted on. Such natural agents uniformly produce their effects and produce them necessarily. And they would so act and produce such effects whether God intended it or not.

Finality in the strict sense means only one thing to Ockham: the freely chosen end for which an intelligent being operates. In the non-intelligent universe he is willing to explain the order which is found there by referring only to a determinism of nature. And it is an intrinsic determinism which points to nothing beyond itself. Fire heats rather than freezes simply because it is fire. Acorns grow into oak trees just because they are acorns. And these things would happen whether God intended them or not. It was not a position which Ockham would have liked to push to its ultimate conclusion. He was much too fond of the divine omnipotence to argue for a physical universe independent of God and coeternal with Him, a universe which could be controlled, perhaps, but never completely subjected to the divine will. Nor is it likely that he had any such idea in mind when he denied that finality could be proved from such a universe. What is behind this denial of finality is much simpler and much more Ockhamistic than that. It is a position which follows logically from his teaching on efficient causality. If efficiency cannot be proved, then neither can finality. And always he means proved from experience or from self-evident principles. And just as efficiency means only association and sequence as far as experi-

---

[17]Ockham, *Quodl. IV*, q. 2: "Intelligitur igitur quaestio de fine primo modo…non potest sufficienter demonstrari nec sciri nec per principia per se nota nec per experientiam quod agens de necessitate naturae agit propter talem causam finalem praestitutam a voluntate; et hoc quia actio talis agentis sine variatione agentis…numquam variatur, sed semper uniformiter sequitur actio; et ideo non potest probari quod tale agens agit propter finem" (OTh IX, 301).

ence can determine, so from these also must any idea of finality be obtained. But if finality means operating for a desired and intended end, there is obviously no evidence of any such intention or desire on the part of the irrational universe. To say, as St. Thomas did, that such regular order and uniform operation demands an intelligent ordering from without was, for Ockham, to go beyond the evidence of experience. Why postulate something extrinsic to explain that which can be explained by something intrinsic?

There is also Ockham's basic attitude to be considered. And this attitude was much more that of the physical scientist than that of the metaphysician. A metaphysician can look at the world and from a single instance of ordered events conclude to an intelligence and from intelligence to its perfection as necessarily existing somewhere. But there is also apparent disorder in the universe. There are operations going on whose purposes we do not know or can only vaguely guess at. In many such instances the farthest we can go is simply to assert the fact when it comes to explaining the physical causes at work. Flowers bloom because they are flowers, and so on. Ockham was content to stop there. And, of course, if one stops there, there is little else to say except that as far as experience shows nature is the final answer.

There is in the physical universe, however—at least as it was understood in the thirteenth and fourteenth centuries—an intelligence at work which we are aware of and which, because it is an intelligence, must operate for an end. That intelligence Ockham calls the "second intelligence," the heavenly body directly responsible for controlling the world. Is it possible from a consideration of this intelligence to conclude to God as its final cause? This, too, according to Ockham is impossible. "It cannot be sufficiently proved that God is the final cause of the second intelligence either in itself or in its effects."[18]

---

[18]Ockham, *Quodl. IV*, q. 2: "Nec potest probari quod Deus sit causa finalis secundae intelligentiae in essendo, quia non potest demonstrari ex per se notis vel per experientiam quod est aliquis effectus a quocumque producibilis nisi effectus quos experimur inter ista inferiora; et per consequens non potest probari quod secunda intelligentia habet causam efficientem, nec per consequens potest probari quod habet causam finalem" (OTh IX, 303).

If we consider the second intelligence in its operation, it is impossible to prove that God is the final cause of such operation. The reason is that, since this intelligence possesses cognitive and volitional faculties, it can set up an end for itself and operate to achieve that end. Neither does it help to consider this being in itself. So considered, the second intelligence has no other end than any natural agent which operates from natural necessity. And if we consider it as operating from natural necessity, there is no need for it to be determined to its effect any more than there is any need for other natural agents to be determined to their effects. All such natural determination comes from the nature of the agent itself. We are back once more to the only possible reason for such natural activity: because it is what it is.

Finally, there is no possibility of demonstrating that God is the final cause of the existence of this second intelligence, since it cannot be demonstrated from self-evident principles or from experience that any being can produce an effect, unless it be an effect which we can experience in an order subject to that being. Now, it cannot be proved that the second intelligence has an efficient cause. Consequently, it cannot be proved that it has a final cause.[19]

The discussion about the possibility of proving that God is the final cause of the physical order is concluded by reaffirming some of the difficulties connected with proving that God is the efficient cause of this order. Just as there could be many first causes in the order of efficiency, so there could be many final causes, each of them adequate in itself and each of them independent of the others. It is quite evident, says Ockham, that a man can go to a tavern to eat and drink. He can go there just as easily to eat or drink. Secondly it is not demonstrable that every ultimate final cause is a necessary being. Just as we ended up with an uncrossable gulf between the first cause and the first being, so here we are faced with the same distance between a final cause and a necessary being. It is simply impossible from a consideration of the forces at work in the physical universe to

---

[19]*Ibid.*

conclude that either the beings themselves or their activities are ordered to a last end which fulfills the definition of God.

Finality and the Human Will

Among the five ways, as St. Thomas presents them, the argument from the finality of the human will is not formally included. Yet it is an aspect of finality in general; and from what St. Thomas has said about the nature of the good and the nature of a natural appetite, it is quite evident that he was aware of and held the validity of such an argument to prove the existence of God. A careful distinction is drawn between an elicited appetite, one which follows upon knowledge, and a natural appetite, which is here nothing else but the natural, dynamic tendency of the will tending toward the supreme good.[20] From the existence of this dynamic tendency toward the supreme good the existence of the supreme good is demanded as that which explains and makes possible such a natural tendency. To deny the existence of a supreme good would be to deny the existence of such a natural tendency. This in turn would be to deny the existence of the human will itself, since the tendency in question is of the essence of such a will. It is impossible to deny that to which the will tends without at the same time denying both the tendency and the will itself. Hence the existential reality of the supreme good is demanded to explain the existential reality of the dynamism of the human will.[21] In syllogistic form the argument is succinctly put as follows: "It is impossible that there exist in man a natural appetite for supreme good, unless that supreme good exists. But there is in man a natural appetite for a supreme good. Therefore the supreme good exists."

The foregoing is a very brief statement of the argument as it is found in St. Thomas. It is not our purpose here to examine it in detail or to consider the difficulties involved. The point is that the argument was familiar to Ockham. It is his attitude toward

---

[20]*Summa Theologiae*, I-II, q. 6, a. 6.

[21]*Summa Theologiae*, I, 12, 1; *SCG*, Bk III.

the argument that is at present under consideration. It is Ockham's difficulties that we want to examine in order to see the source of these difficulties and trace the causes for Ockham's refusal to accept the argument.

In speaking of the fruition toward which the human will tends and which it finds in the good, Ockham distinguished between an ordered and an inordinate fruition.[22] An ordered fruition is had when one loves that which is to be supremely loved with all of his power. An inordinate fruition, on the other hand, is had when one loves supremely and for its own sake that which is meant to be loved less and only for the sake of something else. The ordered fruition can be subdivided into two kinds. One kind is that which simply and completely satisfies the appetite. And this is fruition in the proper sense. The second kind is a fruition which does not simply and completely satisfy the appetite but is rather a love which is not entirely free from anxiety and sadness. This is the only kind we know here on earth.[23] The question is whether it can be naturally demonstrated that a fruition in the proper sense is possible for the human will. Ockham's answer is that the possibility of such a fruition cannot be naturally demonstrated.

In the first place, said Ockham, the philosophers who have diligently examined what is the ultimate end of human activity were not able to conclude that such complete fruition is possible. Hence it does not seem that such possibility is capable of rational proof. Secondly, it is an article of faith that fruition of the divine essence is possible for us, and no article of faith can be rationally demonstrated. Thirdly, it cannot be rationally demon-

---

[22]Ockham, *I Sent.*, d. 1, 94 (OTh I, 431).

[23]Ockham, *Scriptum in I Sent.*, d. 1, q. 4: "...fruitio est duplex, scilicet ordinata et inordinata. Fruitio ordinata est illa quando aliquid summe diligendum summe diligitur. Fruitio inordinata est illa que summe diligitur et propter se quod minus et propter aliud est diligendum. Sed fruitio ordinata est duplex, quia quaedam est quietans simpliciter voluntatem, qualis dicitur esse fruitio patriae; alia non simpliciter quietat, sed permittit secum, etiam naturaliter, anxietatem et tristitiam, qualis est fruitio viae" (OTh I, 431).

strated that no finite good can satisfy the human will. One
argument given is that, since the will is free, it can desire all that
is desirable. But created things never satisfy the human will.
Therefore it goes beyond the created to an uncreated and infinite
good. In answer Ockham replies that it cannot be naturally
demonstrated that the will can freely desire whatever is in itself
desirable, that desiring a finite good necessarily includes the
capacity to desire an infinite good. And this cannot be proved
from the intellect's capacity to apprehend all good. In no sense
does it follow from the intellect's capacity to apprehend all good
that the will can desire all good. It can very possibly be that what
is apprehended in general is never apprehended in particular.
And it is always the particular object which moves the will.
Finally, it cannot be proved that any given act can adequately
bring rest to the will. Since the will is free, it can always turn to
desire something else and will experience sadness if it cannot
possess that something else.[24]

In the first part of this same article Ockham finds still other
reasons to doubt both that a finite object cannot satisfy the
created will and that an uncreated good can satisfy it.

That a finite good can satisfy the human will is shown as follows.
When the acts of some potency are so related to one another that
one is less perfect and another is more perfect, if the less perfect
act can satisfy the potency, much more can the more perfect act
satisfy that same potency. But it is possible that a given act of the

---

[24]Ockham, *Scriptum in I Sent.*, d. 1, q. 4: "...talis fruitio est nobis possibilis non
potest naturaliter probari, videtur, quia philosophi investigantes diligenter quis sit
finis ultimus operum humanorum non potuerunt ad illum finem attingere, igitur
non est verisimile quod hoc possit naturaliter probari...quantum ad istum articulum
primo, quod non potest naturaliter demonstrari quod talis fruitio divinae essentiae
est nobis possibilis, quia istud est mere creditum...Secundo, dico quod non potest
naturaliter demonstrari quod voluntas non potest satiari nec quietari in aliquo citra
Deum...quia non potest naturaliter demonstrari quod voluntas contingenter feratur
in quodlibet volitum...igitur non potest naturaliter probari quod voluntate habente
actum respectu cuiuscumque finiti poterit appetitus seu voluntas appetere perfectius
bonum...non potest naturaliter probari quod voluntas sit per quemcumque actum
quietabilis quin quocumque actu possibili voluntati posito in ipsa voluntate possit
libere velle aliquid aliud et tristari si careat illo" (OTh I, 433).

will with regard to some creature is more perfect and more intense than a given act of the will with regard to God. Even in regard to God the act of the will is a finite act and consequently has a certain proportion by reason of its imperfection to other acts. Hence there seems to be no contradiction involved in saying that there could be another act more perfect than this particular finite act with regard to God. Now, if the act with regard to God is less perfect than some other and, nevertheless, can satisfy the will, much more will that be true of the other act which by supposition is directed toward a creature.[25]

In the second place, Ockham argues that that is to be enjoyed most which is most to be loved. But this can be something else besides God. According to the Philosopher, each one ought to love himself more than anything else. Then, too, if God is that which is to be loved most, the reason is that He is the highest good. Now, the most is to the most as more is to more. Therefore, if the highest good is to be most loved, then the greater good is to be more loved. Consequently, it would follow that an angel is to be more loved by a man than he himself is. Lastly, it is evident that God does not satisfy the human will because the human will can love other things along with God.[26]

In all this argumentation, of course, there is no mention whatever made of the distinction between a natural and an elicited appetite. There is no attempt to distinguish a free act from a

---

[25]Ockham, *Scriptum in I Sent.*, d. 1, q. 4: "…quando aliquis actus alicuius potentiae sic se habent quod unus est simpliciter imperfectior et alius simpliciter perfectior, si actus imperfectior potest satiare potentiam multo magis actus perfectior satiabit eandem. Sed possibile est quod aliquis actus voluntatis respectu alicuius creaturae sit perfectior et intensior quam actus voluntatis respectu Dei, quia cum actus respectu Dei sit finitus et per consequens habeat certam proportionem in perfectione ad alios actus, non videtur includere contradictionem quod fiat aliquis actus perfectior illo actu finito. Igitur si ille actus finitus imperfectior satiat, multo magis alius actus perfectior satiabit. Confirmatur ista ratio, quia si unus actus voluntatis respectu Dei potest satiare voluntatem, igitur actus multiplicati in tantum quod excedant actum voluntatis respectu Dei in perfectione poterunt satiare voluntatem" (OTh I, 429).

[26]*Ibid.*

necessary act. There is no question of an ultimate end in the light of which all means to that end become understandable objects of choice and in the light of which the various choices themselves become intelligible. The will is absolutely free and always remains so even in the face of infinite good. The will can here and now make a more intense act with regard to a creature; therefore, it can be more adequately satisfied by the creature than it can by God. The act of the love of God is a finite act; therefore, it can be compared with all other finite acts. One could grant every statement Ockham makes because all of them miss the essential points of the argument which he is attacking. The reason for this attitude is made clearer in the seventh *Quodlibet,* where Ockham asks whether it can be proved from final causality that God is intrinsically infinite. He holds the opposite because "there is not in the will by nature an appetite for an infinite good."[27]

For a moment we are led to think that Ockham is attacking the very heart of the argument; that he is denying that the will of its very nature is ordered to anything beyond the created. But in the next few sentences it becomes evident that what he means by "natural appetite" is something different. When it is said that a natural inclination is that toward which the will is borne pleasurably and without a previously developed habit, this is true, if such an inclination follows upon a true and not a fictitious concept. It is the nature of the will to follow upon thought—although, since it is free, it is not necessitated; still, the will can be said to be inclined in such a manner only to that which is not the object of a mistaken judgment. This object is not an infinite good. Nor does it follow that although the will can always desire a good greater than every finite good, it naturally desires an infinite good. What the will really desires in such a case is the object of the imagination, which is represented as a greater or lesser good *in infinitum.* There is, in a sense, an appetite for infinite good here, but it is infinite only according to extension. That is, the will can indefinitely desire goods which the imagination presents as greater than the goods which actu-

---

[27]Cf. Ockham, *Scriptum in I Sent.*, d. 1, q. 2 and 6 (OTh I, 394 and 486); Ockham, *Scriptum in IV Sent.*, q. 14 (OTh VII, 278).

ally exist. Such desires, however, follow upon imagination and not upon true concepts.[28] Hence they prove nothing.

Ockham has taken his reply to St. Anselm's argument for the existence of God and transferred it to the realm of volition. It does not follow that God actually exists simply because one must think of Him as that than which no greater exists. Consequently the will's reaction to such a thought does not prove either that God exists. But the objection is valid only when directed against an argument based on an elicited desire. It affects not at all one based on a natural desire.

H. Becher, S.J., traces Ockham's rejection of the argument for the existence of an infinite Good to the absolute freedom of the human will. He summarizes Ockham's attack on the argument as follows. The statement that a finite good cannot fully satisfy the human will can be proved from only three reasons. First, from the freedom of the will it follows that man can strive after everything desirable but can find peace only in the last and highest good. But this argument does not conclude because it cannot be shown to be a contradiction that even a finite good can be willed and striven for necessarily. Then, too, the enjoyment of the infinite good is necessarily a free act.[29] Hence there is really no ultimate good for man. Secondly, the formal object of the will, *bonum in commune,* demands an infinite good. But neither can this be proved. For it is possible to conclude that an essential disproportion can stand between the will and its goal, or an extrinsic cause can hinder the will from an enjoyment and possession of its final end. Thirdly, it cannot be shown that the human will can lay hold of an infinite good, for this is not natural but supernatural. Ultimately, then, finality fails as efficiency had failed to prove conclusively any necessary order in the created world to an ultimate End.

---

[28]Cf. *I Sent.*, 1, 2 and 6; IV Sent., 14 (OTh, as in footnote 27).

[29]Becher, "Gottesbegriff und Gottesbeweis bei Wilhelm Von Ockham," *Scholastik,* 1928, pp. 369-93.

III
Knowledge of the Self and God

 nce Ockham had questioned the validity of the causal proposition, or at least the validity and certainty of any argument grounded on it, serious doubts arose about any knowledge which transcends immediate experience. He had introduced into a world of beings already contingent in their being a more drastic contingency affecting their natures and their operations. It is true that in doing so he had opened a way for God to act in that world with a freedom which far surpassed that recognized by previous philosophers and theologians. But his very success in achieving that would lead Ockham down a path which limited more and more the area of demonstrative knowledge. Ockham was quite willing to accept the consequences.

Knowledge of the Self
Introduction

In Question 87 of the *Summa Theologiae* St. Thomas wrote the following:

> The intellect knows itself, not by its essence but by its act. This happens in two ways: in the first place, singularly, as when Socrates or Plato perceives that he has an intellectual soul because he perceives that he understands.

He indicates that there is a second kind of knowledge of the intellectual soul which is universal in nature and which is derived from a knowledge of the intellectual act. This requires a careful and subtle inquiry. For the first kind of knowledge, however, there is only required the presence of the mind to itself.

> The mere presence of the mind suffices for the first; since the mind itself is the principle of action whereby it perceives itself by its own presence.[1]

Less than a century later William of Ockham could write the following:

> If we understand by the intellectual soul an immaterial and incorruptible form which is totally in the whole and totally in each part, we cannot know either through reason or experience that we possess such a form.[2]

He adds that he cares not what Aristotle said about this because he seems to be doubtful about it himself. Ockham accepts the very existence of such an intellectual and incorruptible soul only on faith. The radical change in the position taken by Ockham is startling.

The Object of Knowledge

It seems that if anyone could be immediately aware of the presence in man of an intellectual soul, that person was William of Ockham. In order to safeguard the certainty of human knowing he had carefully distinguished between intuitive and abstract knowledge. He rejected the Thomistic contention that the

---

[1]*S.Th.*, I, 87, 1.

[2]Ockham, *Quodl. I*, q. 10: "Quantum ad secundam difficultatem, dico quod intelligendo per 'animam intellectivam' formam immaterialem, incorruptibilem quae tota est in toto corpore et tota in qualibet parte, nec potest evidenter sciri per rationem vel per experientiam quod talis forma sit in nobis, nec quod intelligere tali substantiae proprium sit in nobis, nec quod talis anima sit forma corporis,— quidquid de hoc senserit Philosophus non curo ad praesens, quia ubique dubitative videtur loqui—, sed ista tria solum credimus" (OTh IX, 63).

universal is known intellectually prior to the singular in which it is grounded. If this were so, what possible certitude could be had for the objectivity of such a universal? But if the existing singular is known first, the ground for existential objectivity is there. Not only is this true of material singulars existing outside the mind, but it is also true of those acts of the intellect and will which we elicit. They, too, can become by a reflexive act immediate objects of our knowledge. Such knowledge depends on a previous act of intuition of the object of such acts of knowing, affection, joy, etc., but the intellect can turn directly to the interior act and apprehend it intuitively.

> The mind can know intuitively some things which are interior, for example, acts of intellection and willing and delight independently of the senses, ... although some other intuitive knowledge is presupposed.[3]

He is, however, careful to add that such intuitions are only of the acts, not of habits or other intelligibles in the soul.

Now one could leap to a facile conclusion based on Ockham's insistence that every reality is a unique singular and that from one such singular another cannot be known. Hence, the argument could be made that, since each act of the soul is a singular act, one is not justified in asserting the existence of the soul as the subject of the act. After all, the act is not the soul, and, as is well known, God by His absolute power is able to sustain any act independent of its object or its source. But it is not that simple, as we shall see.

The World of Singulars

It is a well known fact that Ockham had little use for any sort of Platonic approach to reality. The world is a collection of unique

---

[3]Ockham, *Quodl. I*, q. 14: "Utrum intellectus noster pro statu isto cognoscat actus suos intuitive...dico quod sic. Quia de cognitione intellectus et volitione formatur prima propositio contingens quia evidenter cognoscitur ab intellectu, puta talis 'intellectio est, volitio est'" (OTh IX, 78).

singulars which are grasped intuitively by both sense and intellect. These singulars are unique to such an extent that there are no real relations connecting one with another. Peter is similar to John, for example, simply because he is Peter and John is John. He interprets Aristotle to mean that such relations exist only in the mind and in no way outside it. Even in the mind relations are simply connotative terms which are used to signify two actual existents which are uniquely themselves. The world, then, is a collection of absolutes none of which ever necessarily demands another. There is, therefore, no way in which one could proceed from the knowledge of one thing to the knowledge of the existence of another. Concepts are also just as independent of each other as are the things themselves. As a matter of fact, the knowledge of a thing itself could be had independently of the thing. One need only recall here his teaching on the knowledge of non-existents.[4]

Man and Soul

Ockham treats of man in a physical and material context, but he makes the distinctions which are necessary for a Christian theologian. Like all other material beings man is composed of matter and form. This material principle, unlike Aristotle's, has an existence in its own right. It is not pure potentiality, but even as matter is a reality.[5] Its potentiality is only toward the various forms which will inform it. The first of these forms is that of corporeality which makes it a body and which it retains until

---

[4]Ockham, *Quodl. I*, q. 13 (Oth IX, 72); *Quodl. VI*, q. 6 (OTh IX, 604).

[5]*Physics* I, 7. "Et primo de materia. Circa quam est sciendum quod materia est quaedam res actualiter existens in rerum natura, quae est in potentia ad omnes formas substantiales, nullam habens necessario semper sibi inhaerentem et inexistentem. Et ideo non est imaginandum quod materia sit quid in potentia tantum de se.... Sed materia est vere actu ex seipsa ita quod per nullam virtutem potest esse in potentia ad esse in rerum natura...licet semper sit in potentia ad formam qua privatur." Cf. Leff, Gordon, *William of Ockham* (Rowman and Littlefield, Totowa, NJ, 1975), p. 573, footnote 47.

this body itself decomposes. For even when the sensible and intellectual forms have departed, man still remains a body recognizable as such. The second form in man is that of sensitivity. This form is really distinct from that of corporeality and provides the body with its animal characteristics and powers. It is an extended form, as is obvious from its different functions in different areas of matter. It functions differently, for example, in the eye than it does in the ear, etc. Hence, its extension throughout the body is obvious. That it is really distinct from both the form of corporeality and the intellectual form is equally clear. The first remains when the sensitive form has corrupted, and at times, at least, it plays a role contrary to that of the intellectual form. For the sensitive form can desire an object in direct contradiction to that of the intellectual form. Such opposite activities cannot possibly be in the same species.[6]

When we come to the intellectual form, we find an entirely different reality. Such a form is not quantitative, and it is, therefore, not extended but *tota in qualibet parte totius.*[7] It is, furthermore, spiritual, incorruptible, immortal, and the form of the body. But, as we shall see, there is no way to demonstrate this philosophically, but it must be held only on faith. These three forms, all informing matter, constitute the unique unity which is man. And although Ockham insisted on this numerical unity, he does seem to be in difficulty here. His criterion for a real distinction was always separability. He rejected the Thomistic doctrine of a real distinction between principles which were not separable. He had also rejected the Scotistic distinction of distinct formalities in the unity of the same being. But the three forms in man are obviously separable, as he had previously pointed out. Hence, he could do nothing else but admit their distinction as separate realities and at the same time insist on the numerical unity of the individual man. It is here, perhaps, that his position becomes as weak as it ever does. It is difficult to conceive how man remains a numerical unity composed as he is of four different and separable realities.

---

[6]Ockham, *Quodl. II*, q. 10: "Utrum anima sensitiva et intellectiva in homine distinguantur realiter" (OTh IX, 156).

[7]*Quodlibet I*, 10. (OThIX, 62).

Form and its Powers

If, however, there is a real distinction between the forms themselves, there is no such distinction between a form and its
powers. It is true that we speak of a difference between seeing
and hearing and between intellect and will, as well as between
the acts of knowing and willing. But these are connotative terms
which are useful in speaking of such operations. In reality they
point to no such real distinctions. The soul sensing is identical
with what we designate as sense operations. The soul knowing
and willing is simply the soul in act which expresses itself in
various ways. The distinctions are all on the side of the mind
which distinguishes in order to clarify. One could just as easily
say that the soul knows by its will and wills by its intellect.[8] At
this point the problem which confronts Ockham is this. He had
granted that there is an immediate intuition of existing material
things as well as an immediate intuition of the acts of the
intellect and will. If one can directly intuit an act of knowing, for
example, and if this act of knowing is identical with the intellectual soul, why cannot he also admit an intuition of the intellectual
soul? Why cannot he agree with Aquinas that the soul knows
itself in knowing its act?

The Act and its Source

In the first place, in accord with his principle of economy
Ockham had refused to multiply powers and acts as really
distinct from their source. All such distinctions were merely
connotative. In the second place, each intuition regards its
immediate object and nothing else. From the knowledge of one
reality we can never argue to the existence of another. This
would require an habitual knowledge of the other, and in the
present case we are speaking of an original knowledge of the soul
for which there has been no previous knowledge. On this ground
any transition from one knowledge to another is ruled out. In
addition he had already made it clear that God by His absolute

---

[8]Ockham, *II Sent.*, 24, L. (Lyons, 1495). Not found in critical edition.

power could sustain an act of knowing independently of the existence of its ordinary object. There is no reason why this cannot be applied equally to the source of the act. In the third place, his theory of causality presents a real difficulty. While, as we have seen, he was willing to admit that there was causality at work in the world, he could never argue from the existence of a particular effect to the existence of a particular cause. Again God could well be the cause, or at least some agent of whose existence we are totally unaware. Ockham grants only an intuition of the act itself. That intuition can go no further. Hence, even if one can present plausible reasons for the identity of the act and its source, that source simply does not show up in the act. And no case can be presented for the existence of something which cannot be directly intuited. The certain existence of such a source, then, must be held on faith. And if such a source cannot be demonstrated philosophically, then nothing about its function in the human individual can be demonstrated. It might well function as a form. But it might also function simply as a mover. How could anyone possibly know?

In the tenth question of the first *Quodlibet* Ockham treats the problem directly. It seems possible to demonstrate, he says, that the intellectual soul is the form of the body. We experience intellection in us. This intellection is an operation of man. Therefore, its efficient cause and source is also in us. Furthermore, this cannot be some separated intelligence because we could in no way experience the operations of such an intelligence. Hence, the subject of such an operation must be in man. Now it cannot be the matter; therefore, it must be the form.

Immediately, however, he sees two difficulties. The first is that the intellectual soul could be that through which we understand and still not be the form of the body. We could simply be attributing the term, form, to such a principle, as we attribute the term, rower, to one who rows. The soul could be a mover rather than the proper form of the body. In that case we could still say that man understands through his intellectual soul. In the second place, he states flatly that neither through experience nor reason can we know that a spiritual principle which we call the soul exists in us. We hold this solely on faith. And even if we

directly experience acts of knowing and willing and believe
through faith that the subject of such acts is spiritual and
incorruptible, still we could just as well conclude from experience that the subject of such acts is an extended and corruptible
form.[9]

Conclusion

It is interesting to note that some four hundred years later David
Hume could write the following on the identity of the self.

> When I turn my reflection on myself, I can never perceive this
> self without some one or more perceptions; nor can I ever
> perceive anything but the perceptions. It is the composition of
> these, therefore, which forms the self.
>
> We can conceive a thinking being to have either many or few
> perceptions. Suppose the mind to be reduced even below the
> life of an oyster. Suppose it to have only one perception, as of
> thirst or hunger. Consider it in that situation. Do you conceive
> anything but merely that perception? Have you any notion of
> self or substance? If not, the addition of other perceptions can
> never give you that notion.
>
> The annihilation, which some people suppose to follow upon
> death, and which entirely destroys this self, is nothing but an
> extinction of all particular perceptions; love and hatred, pain
> and pleasure, thought and sensation. These, therefore, must be
> the same with the self; since the one cannot survive the
> other.[10]

---

[9]*Quodlibet I*, 10. "Sunt etiam aliqua dubia quia videtur quod anima intellectiva
quam ponimus secundum fidem informare corpus non sit tota in toto, nec tota in
qualibet parte.... Ad principale renderent sequentes rationes naturales, quod
experimur intellectionem in nobis qui est actus formae corruptibilis et corporeae.
Et diceret consequenter quod talis intellectio recipietur in forma extensa. Non
autem experimur istam intellectionem quae est operatio propria substantiae
immaterialis. Et ideo per intellectionem non concludimus illam substantiam
incorruptibilem esse in nobis tamquam formam" (OTh IX, 62).

[10]Hume, David, *A Treatise of Human Nature*, Part Iv, Section 6.

It would be easy to say at this point that, when Ockham and Hume had finished their analyses of man, man had lost both his unity and his soul. But, of course, there is more to it than that. Ockham was not just a philosopher, but much more radically a theologian and a Christian. And like any Augustinian Christian theologian he was interested in pointing out the inadequacy of human reason when left to itself or when dealing with the empirical situation. The *ratio inferior* was just that. Unless it was subjected to the *ratio superior*, enlightened by faith and the Divine Light Itself, there was very little that human reason working by itself could achieve in the way of certain truth. Aristotle was there, and to a certain extent he accepted him. But to pretend that man in his present condition could find salvation and ultimate truth through the teachings of the Stagirite was simply nonsense. What after all were faith and grace meant for, if not to sustain a darkened human intellect and a wayward will, and raise them to the level where man could truly and really understand and consistently pursue the good? In Ockham's eyes Christianity was not just something superadded to an already noble reason. It was rather that without which man could never understand himself, his world, or his God with any degree of certitude whatever. The conclusion to so many questions is consistently the same: "This we hold only by faith."

Ockham, then, does not abdicate certitude. He is simply unable to find very much of it on the philosophical level. He is convinced of this, and this conviction is behind all his criticism of Aquinas, Scotus, Henry of Ghent, *et al*. In the end Ockham is much more an Augustinian than he is a sceptic. He has been called often enough a philosophical sceptic, and from that abstract viewpoint he was. But it is also true that Ockham himself would not welcome such a designation as a total description of his work. He never stopped with a philosophical scepticism. He uses it to point to where man must go, if he is to achieve the certitude he seeks. If an empiricist is unwilling to go beyond his empiricism, then the result, in Ockham's mind, is quite clear. And it seems that historically he has been right. The quotation from Hume represents Hume's total position. It is not Ockham's.

Knowledge of God

Can God Be Known by Human Reason?

That God could be known by human reason, or better, perhaps, by human mind, was never doubted by Ockham. There are truths which man must know, if he is to save his soul; and some of these necessary truths can be known naturally, such as that God exists, that He is wise and good, and so on.[11] Furthermore, we can talk about God; we use a special name to designate Him, and that name is validly imposed. To name a thing it is sufficient to know that thing as being distinct from everything else. This is certainly possible for the human mind with regard to God.[12] Against the objection that to know a thing one has to know clearly what the name signifies, Ockham replied that "clearly" here means only that the name can refer to God and to nothing else. But there are many such names which can refer only to God and which we use constantly. In this sense, then, there are names which clearly signify God, but there are behind those names concepts which can be properly applied to God.[13] As we shall see later, it is the nature of such concepts which causes the difficulty. However that may be, one thing is immediately evident; namely, that there is no concept which results from an immediate apprehension of the divine essence. "God cannot be known

---

[11]Ockham, *Quaestio Prima Principalis Prologi*, F.: "Circa tertium dico omnes veritates necessariae homini viatori ad aeternam beatitudinem consequendam sunt veritates theologicae.... Ex isto sequitur quod aliquae veritates naturaliter notae seu cognoscibiles sunt theologicae, sicut quod Deus est, Deus est sapiens, bonus etc." (OTh I, 7).

[12]Ockham, *Scriptum in I Sent.*, d. 22, q. 1: "Utrum viator possit aliquod nomen imponere ad distincte significandum divinam essentiam?...quod significat Deum et nihil aliud, distincte Deum significat; sed multa nomina Deum significant et nihil aliud...et illa sunt imposita a viatore" (OTh IV, 45).

[13]Ockham, *Scriptum in I Sent.*, d. 22, q. 1: "...viator potest imponere nomen ad distincte significandum Deum vel divinam essentiam. Hoc patet quia quicumque potest vere intelligere aliquid esse distinctum ab alio, potest instituere nomen ad illud distincte significandum. Sed viator potest vere intelligere et scire Deum esse distinctum ab omni alio, igitur etc." (OTh IV, 55).

in Himself in such a way that the Divine essence would terminate the act of understanding immediately, without anything else concurring as an object."[14]

Such a knowledge of God by direct apprehension would make it impossible for anyone to doubt the existence of God. And this is obviously against the facts. Furthermore, such a concept would be one of two kinds, either intuitive or abstractive. It could not be intuitive, since such a concept is reserved for the blessed. Nor does it help to say that it is an abstract concept, since every abstraction supposes an intuition.[15]

In the *Prologue to the Sentences* Ockham admits the possibility of an exception to this rule, for he states that an abstractive and distinctive knowledge of God is possible even here on earth and can be communicated by God to the *viator* independently of any previous intuition of the Godhead. It is true that intuitive knowledge is an essential cause of any abstract knowledge, but it is only an extrinsic cause. And whatever God can do through the mediation of an extrinsic cause, He can also do immediately and alone. He could, therefore, communicate to the *viator* an abstractive knowledge of Himself without a previously communicated intuitive knowledge. Only this last is absolutely impossible for the person who does not as yet possess the beatific vision.[16] Gabriel Biel in his commentary on the matter states

---

[14]Ockham, *Scriptum in I Sent.*, d. 2, q. 9: "...Deus non potest cognosci in se, ita quod ipsamet divina essentia terminet immediate actum intelligendi, nullo alio concurrente in ratione obiecti" (OTh II, 312).

[15]*Ibid.*

[16]Ockham, *Quaest. Prima,* I, 2: "...dico quod Deus, de potentia Dei absoluta, potest tali duplici notitia cognosci, ita quod una sit intuitiva et alia abstractiva...si abstractiva non posset esse sine intuitiva Dei, igitur intuitiva esset causa essentialis respectu abstractiva, sed non nisi extrinseca: et quidquid potest Deus mediante causa extrinseca, potest immediate per se. Igitur potest facere abstractivam sine intuitiva et e converso...ex praedictis concludo quod notitia deitatis distincta est communicabilis viatori, manenti viatori, quia sola intuitiva repugnat viatori. Igitur si abstractiva potest fieri sine intuitiva, sequitur quod abstractiva notitia distincta deitatis potest esse in viatore, manente viatore" (OTh I, 48).

that Ockham is speaking here of something that could only take place supernaturally, as is evident from the words *per potentiam divinam.* Naturally such a knowledge—abstractive without a previous intuition—is impossible.[17]

Can God Be Known by a Proper Concept?

Secondly, we cannot know God by means of a concept which is proper to Him alone and simple in its nature. Such a concept presupposes that the object has been previously and inductively known.[18] What is the nature, then, of this concept of God which lies behind the various names we use to designate Him? In speaking of the first object of the human intellect Ockham makes a distinction between that which lies behind and is known in every predication about a *per se* intelligible and that which is the most perfect object of the intellect.[19] God does not terminate our act of understanding. That is a material quiddity. Neither is it the concept of God which lies behind every predication and makes every predication intelligible. Everything that is known is known either in itself or in a concept proper to it or in some other kind of concept. In our present state God is not

---

[17]Biel, Gabriel, "Dicitur per potentiam divinam, quia naturaliter impossible...," *Collectorium circa quattuor libros Sentientiarum,* Werbeck, W. and Hofmann, U., eds., Tübingen: J.C.B. Mohr, 1973, p. 16.

[18]Ockham, *Scriptum in I Sent.,* d. 2, q. 9: "...quod nihil potest cognosci a nobis ex puris naturalibus in conceptu simplici sibi proprio nisi ipsum in se praecognoscatur. Ista patet inductive" (OTh II, 314).

[19]Ockham, *Scriptum in I Sent.,* d. 3, q. 1: "Et primo distinguo de primo obiecto intellectus, quia quoddam potest intelligi esse primum objectum intellectus vel primitate generationis, et est illud quod terminat primum actum intelligendi; vel potest esse primum primitate adaequationis, et tunc esset illud quod praedicaretur de omnibus per se intelligibilibus, qualiter tamen hoc esset intelligendum, dictum est prius; vel potest esse primum primitate perfectionis, et est perfectissimum intelligibile ab intellectu. Secundo dico quod Deus non est primum cognitum a nobis" (OTh II, 388).

known to us as He is in Himself. The reason is that God is not known to us in particular nor in His own proper nature.[20]

Considering an objection, Ockham becomes still clearer. The objection cited is one which takes the position that the knowledge of God from creatures is of two kinds. The first kind is a knowledge which is associated with the prime notions of being, the *primae intentiones entis.* The second is a rational and deductive knowledge. Speaking of the second type of knowledge the objector and Ockham admit that in this sense God is the last object of the intellect and not the first. Of the first type of knowledge, which includes the concept of God among the first notions possessed naturally by the human mind, a proof is submitted. Just as the senses proceed naturally from the less determined to the more determined, from body to animal to man and to this man, so the intellect proceeds from an indeterminate knowledge of being to a more determinate knowledge of this being. The more indetermined an intelligible is, the sooner it is known by the intellect. As it becomes less indetermined and more restricted, more and more acts of the intellect are required. And since, as far as we are concerned, God is most indetermined, He is the first object known by the human intellect. Ockham's answer to this objection is a simple denial that our cognitive process follows such a course. He asserts on the contrary that intellection begins with the singular.[21]

---

[20]Ockham, *Scriptum in I Sent.,* d. 3, q. 1: "Primum patet, quia omnis res, si cognoscatur, vel cognoscitur in se, vel cognitione propria sibi vel aequivalenti, vel in aliquo conceptu. Sed Deus non cognoscitur primo in se a nobis pro statu isto: tum quia Deus non cognoscitur a nobis in particulari et in natura propria; tum quia omnis notitia rei in se abstractiva naturaliter adquisita praesupponit intuitivam" (OTh II, 389).

[21]Ockham, *Scriptum in I Sent.,* d. 3, q. 1: "...cognitio Dei ex creaturis duplex est, scilicet naturalis et rationalis. Prima est cognitio Dei cum primis intentionibus entis concepta statim et naturaliter. Secunda est via ratiocinativae deductionis animadversa. Loquendo de ista secunda cognitione, 'quid est Deus' non est primum quod homo cognoscit ex creaturis, sed ultimum. Loquendo primo modo, dicitur quod 'quid est Deus' est primum cognitum a nobis naturaliter" (OTh II, 381). Such a knowledge is, of course, confused and does not distinguish God from the "primae intentiones Entis."

If this is true, there is only one possibility left for the human mind to acquire some knowledge of God, and that is by way of singular, created objects. Ockham sums up his position as follows:

> Everything that is knowable by us is known either in itself, or in a concept which is simple and proper to that thing, or in a concept which is complex but still proper to that object, or, finally, in a concept which is common to the object and other things as well.[22]

We have already seen him rule out the first two types of concept. The third is also rejected because such a complex but still proper concept would merely be a composition of simple and proper concepts. Hence, all that remains is that God can be known in and by means of a concept which is common to Him and other things as well. Nevertheless, this concept of God is not merely an extrinsic denomination, but a real, quidditative concept. Ockham reasons as follows. This concept is either quidditative or denominative. If we suppose that it is denominative, then that to which the concept is attributed is itself either quidditative or denominative. And so on to infinity. But such an infinite process is impossible. Therefore, the concept must be quidditative.

This quidditative concept of God is not, however, an analogous one. Against Henry of Ghent Ockham argues that to posit an analogous concept of God is to posit a proper concept of Him. He takes proper here to mean a concept which not only refers to God alone—he will admit such a proper concept of God—but one which gives us some knowledge of what God is in Himself. His

---

[22]Ockham, *Scriptum in I Sent.*, d. 2, q. 9: "...omne cognoscibile a nobis aut cognoscitur in se, aut in conceptu simplici sibi proprio, aut in conceptu composito proprio, aut in conceptu communi sibi et aliis...aut ille conceptus est quidditativus aut denominativus? Si quidditativus, habetur propositum. Si denominativus, tunc quaero de illo cui attribuis istum conceptum denominativum: aut est denominativus, et erit processus in infinitum, aut quidditativus, et habetur propositum" (OTh II, 325).

reason for rejecting such a proper concept of God is precisely the same as that for rejecting an analogous concept of God. An analogous concept of God would mean that God was known in particular. And that is impossible.[23] Neither the divine essence nor anything intrinsic to the Godhead can be known by us in such a way that nothing else is present in the object, for that would mean intuition of God.[24]

The Quidditative Concept of God

What does quidditative mean, then, and in what sense is a proper concept of God possible for the human mind? Ockham defines the God-concept simply as a concept which is both proper and composite and one whose parts are able to be abstracted naturally from things.[25] Just as the creatures can be known in some note which is common and simple, so also can God, because otherwise He would be completely unknowable. Now, when there are many things all having the same note in common, those many things refer back properly to that thing which possesses that common note as its distinguishing characteristic and to it alone; for the other things have their distinguishing characteristics which differentiate them from one another. Hence all those things can refer back only to that one thing in whose characteristic note they share. Now, there are many concepts that are simple and can be abstracted naturally, any one of which is proper to God and creatures. But since many creatures share

---

[23]Ockham, *Scriptum in I Sent.*, d. 3, q. 2 (OTh II, 393).

[24]Ockham, *Scriptum in I Sent.*, d. 3, q. 2: "...nec divina essentia, nec divina quidditas, nec aliquid intrinsecum Deo, nec aliquid quod est realiter Deus potest in se cognosci a nobis, ita quod nihil aliud a Deo concurrat in ratione obiecti" (OTh II, 402).

[25]Ockham, *Scriptum in I Sent.*, d. 3, q. 2: "Secundo, dico quod essentia divina vel quidditas divina potest cognosci a nobis in aliquo conceptu sibi proprio, composito tamen, et hoc in conceptu cuius partes sunt abstrahibiles naturaliter a rebus" (OTh II, 402).

these concepts they refer back always to that object whose distinguishing characteristic they are. And when combined, all these concepts make one complex concept which is proper to God alone. And since it can be known that that concept can be verified with regard to an object whose characteristic note it is, God can be known in that concept. For example, from many beings a concept of being can be abstracted which is proper to God and to all other things. In the same way there can be an abstract concept of wisdom. The same is true of the concept of goodness, insofar as the concept of goodness is distinguished from that of wisdom. Yet every such concept can be properly verified only with regard to God, and to Him alone will the combination of concepts properly refer. He alone is wisdom, goodness, and being.

This should not be taken as a proof for God's existence, a proof based on participated perfection. It is no such thing. Ockham is not arguing from participated formal perfections to the existence of the All-Perfect. He is dealing only in concepts and is saying only that the concepts which the mind abstracts from creatures can be applied to something we call God. Whether that something exists or not is not his concern here. It is simply a question of what we can know about the nature of God. The concept common to many in its origin can now refer only to God. The aggregate of concepts can be predicated only of God. Yet each concept has come originally from creatures. It is quidditative in the sense that it tells us something about the nature of the creature. It is composite in the sense that it is based on the union of many individual concepts of many singulars. Yet when predicated of God, it is also a proper concept, for it can now refer only to God and to nothing else.[26]

---

[26]Ockham, *I Sent.* d. 3, q. 2: "...sicut creatura potest cognosci in conceptu aliquo communi simplici, ita potest Deus, quia aliter nullo modo esset a nobis cognoscibilis. Sed nunc est ita quod quando sunt multa communia habentia aliquod idem contentum, omnia illa communia simul accepta faciunt unum proprium illi, quia ex quo sunt distincta communia, oportet quod aliquid contineatur sub singulo quod sub nullo aliorum continetur, igitur omnia illa communia simul accepta nulli alii possunt convenire. Sed nunc est ita quod sunt multi conceptus simplices naturaliter abstrahibiles quorum quilibet est communis Deo et alicui alteri, igitur omnes illi

We can ask here whether this concept is also quidditative in the sense that it tells us something of what God is in Himself. Is it really God whom we know, or is it only this aggregate of concepts which we have formed from creatures? There is no hesitation in Ockham's answer.

> I say that we cannot know in itself either the unity of God, or His primacy, or His infinity, or His power, or His goodness, or any other divine perfection. That which we know directly is some concepts which are really not God, but which we use in the propositions we formulate about God.[27]

Such an answer is fully in accord with Ockham's theory of cognition. In another place he states clearly that any science is about propositions, for these are the objects of the science and only these are known.[28] I do not think that Ockham is saying that

---

simul accepti facient unum conceptum proprium Deo, et ita cum possit cognosci quod ille conceptus de aliquo verificatur, Deus in illo conceptu cognoscetur. Verbi gratia, ab entibus potest abstrahi conceptus entis qui est communis Deo et omnibus aliis entibus, similiter potest abstrahi conceptus sapientiae qui est praecise communis sapientiae increatae et sapientiae creatae, similiter potest abstrahi conceptus bonitatis qui est praecise communis bonitati divinae et bonitati creatae, et hoc secundum quod bonitas distinguitur a sapientia, et omnes isti conceptus simul non poterunt verificari nisi de solo Deo, ex quo, per positum, nulla sapientia creata est bonitas creata nec e converso. Et ita cum possit concludi quod aliquod ens est bonitas et sapientia et sic de aliis, quae vocantur attributa, sequitur quod Deus isto modo cognoscitur in conceptu composito sibi proprio. Et hoc non est aliud nisi a creaturis abstrahere multos conceptus communes Deo et creaturis, et concludere particulariter de uno conceptu simplici communi sibi et aliis unum conceptum compositum proprium Deo" (OTh II, 403).

[27]Ockham, *Scriptum in I Sent.* d. 3, q. 2: "...dico quod nec unitatem Dei, nec primitatem, nec infinitam potentiam, nec bonitatem, nec perfectionem divinam possumus in se cognoscere, sed illa quae immediate cognoscimus sunt aliqui conceptus qui non sunt Deus realiter, quibus tamen utimur in propositionibus pro Deo, vel cognoscimus cognitione communi plura quam Deum, et ideo illa unitas quae est Deus vel potentia vel perfectio simpliciter quae est Deus non potest a nobis cognosci in se" (OTh II, 413).

[28]Ockham, *Scriptum in I Sent.*, d. 2, q. 4 (OTh II, 99).

all knowledge is restricted to a knowledge of propositions or of concepts. He would certainly insist that the propositions which are known are verified in reality in this or that existing singular. This existing object, however, is known by an intuition. Once we get beyond the realm of the intuitive apprehension and pass over into the realm of the judgment, the object of that judgment—or, better, the truth it expresses—does not exist as a concrete singular but as an object in the mind at which the mind terminates. And one of the modern commentators on Ockham makes it still clearer. His reason for positing intuition of the existing singular was an attempt to reach certain knowledge of an existing world. He regarded the judgment as a mere combining of concepts and an abstract concept in itself as an object of knowledge.

> Thus we see the problem of intuitive cognition being located at the very heart of the problem of certitude. For Ockham in effect is asking himself: How can I be sure of the truth of contingent propositions? ... For example, if all I have is a concept of whiteness and a concept of Socrates, how can I ever combine these two concepts and know for sure that Socrates is white? A type of cognition which abstracts from existential qualifications of the subject would never suffice for an evident proposition about the existential facts of that subject. Therefore to explain the fact of evident cognition of contingent facts, we must posit another type of cognition which gives us precisely what abstractive cognition ignores; namely, the existential qualifications of things, their *hic* and *nunc*.[29]

Everything except the intuition of the here and now existing singular is for Ockham an abstract concept, and it is about this concept that he philosophizes. Being, the subject of metaphysics, is a concept of the mind,[30] and hence his metaphysics becomes necessarily a science of essences and possibilities. All knowledge of existence is limited to a knowledge of the empirical world of creatures because intuition is limited to such a

---

[29]S. Day, O.F.M., *Intuitive Cognition: A Key to the Significance of the Later Scholastics* (St. Bonaventure, NY: Franciscan Institute, 1947).

[30]Ockham, *Scriptum in III Sent.*, q. 9 (OTh VI, 276).

world. As we have seen, Ockham had drawn a clear distinction between this intuitive knowledge and abstract knowledge. Having ruled out all intuitive knowledge of God, only abstract knowledge was left. Even here the object of such abstract knowledge is not God but the creature, and even the creature is only a secondary object. The primary object is the concept itself, for there is nothing in the experiential order corresponding to such a concept taken as such. The God-concept is in a sense objectified and stands apart from creatures on the one side, too perfect in its composition to be identified with any of them, and distinct from God on the other side, too imperfect and abstract to give us any real knowledge of what He is like. Such a concept is a logical construct which stands for God and tells me all that I shall ever know about Him.

The Univocity of the God-Concept

Now it is one thing to say that we cannot know God as He is in Himself and quite another to say that all we know is a concept of God taken from creatures. Ockham had rejected all analogy and had made the predication of being a univocal one.[31] He could divide the concept of being into two main species, one of which was the created, the other the uncreated. It is well to note here that he never meant to suggest that the reality itself was univocal. God is not being as creatures are being. But Ockham thought that, unless the concept were univocal, the human mind could never come to a knowledge of God. For Ockham the world was not just a collection of singular existents but a collection of absolute and independent existents, none of which had any necessary connection with any other. Again he did not deny that such a connection did in fact exist, but it need not; and as far as our knowledge went such a connection could not be

---

[31]Ockham, *Scriptum in I Sent.*, d. 2, q. 9 (OTh II, 292).

demonstrated.[32] From the knowledge of one such singular existent no one could infer the existence of any other thing. But
when one does become aware of the existence of other things, he
could not know them unless he were able to apply to them a term
which is common to these other things and the ones he already
knows.[33]

When it comes to God, then, unless there is a concept which in
some way, at least, refers to both God and creatures, God could
never be known from creatures. He posited, therefore, a univocal
predication of such concepts as being, wisdom, and goodness
with regard to God and creatures. An analogous predication,
thought Ockham, would lead to one of two unanswerable
difficulties. Either God would be exiled completely from the
realm of human knowledge, or we would end up with a proper
concept of the Godhead. In every analogy there is something
which is the same and something which is different. If the first
is insisted upon, we should arrive at a concept of God which was
proper to Him as such. If the second were insisted upon, then a
concept such as being, for example, would be predicated in a
manner completely different of God and creatures.

So Ockham chose univocity and a concept of being which could
be predicated univocally of God and creatures, at least to the
extent that the concept was common to both in two respects.
God and creatures were alike in this, that they were not nothing;
and, secondly, whatever degrees of existential perfection any
creature possessed, God also possessed that same perfection.

---

[32]Ockham, *Prologus ad Commentarium in Sent.*, I, 1: "Ex istis sequitur quod notitia
intuitiva, tam sensitiva quam intellectiva, potest esse de re non exsistente. Et hanc
conclusionem probo, aliter quam prius, sic: omnis res absoluta, distincta loco et
subiecto ab alia re absoluta, potest per divinam potentiam absolutam exsistere sine
illa, quia non videtur verisimile quod si Deus vult destruere unam rem absolutam
exsistentem in caelo quod necessitetur destruere unam aliam rem exsistentem in
terra. Sed visio intuitiva, tam sensitiva quam intellectiva, est res absoluta, distincta
loco et subiecto ab obiecto. Sicut si videam intuitive stellam exsistentem in caelo,
illa visio intuitiva, sive sit sensitiva sive intellectiva, distinguitur loco et subiecto
ab obiecto viso; igitur ista visio potest manere stella destructa" (OTh I, 38).

[33]Ockham, *Scriptum in III Sent.*, q. 9 (OTh VI, 276).

Ockham had chosen univocity primarily as a means of avoiding an unknown God.

At the same time, to avoid being accused of pantheistic inclinations, he had to make the fact clear that in the real order God and creatures were essentially different. The univocal concept, then, which was predicated of God and creatures did not really signify God; for univocal concepts, as St. Thomas says, are restricted to those things which participate in the same genus.[34] But God belongs in no genus. Hence all that Ockham could eventually say was that he had a concept of God taken from creatures. This concept as a composite of creaturely perfections could refer only to God. Yet, when broken down into its component parts, the concept really said nothing more about God than about the various creatures from which it came. It simply said more perfections, not greater perfections. An analogous concept says something about its object. In this case a univocal concept says nothing about its object but merely stands for that object; and Ockham admits as much. A concept is quidditative, he says, in respect to something which stands for the quiddity and not in respect to something else which is merely denominated from the quiddity. In the proposition that God is wisdom, wisdom stands for the Godhead, which is not a subject.[35] The real subject is the creature from which Ockham first understood the meaning of wisdom. When this wisdom is predicated of God, it is still created wisdom at least as far as the meaning goes—and one knows no more about the divine wisdom than one did before making the predication. Only the concept of human wisdom is known, and behind that stands infinite wisdom, untouched by the human intellect, unknown, and incapable of being known. The same is true of all the other perfections predicated of God.

---

[34]*Summa Contra Gentiles*, I, cap. 32.

[35]Ockham, *Scriptum in I Sent.*, d. 3, q. 3: "...omnis ille conceptus est quidditativus respectu alicuius qui primo supponit pro ipsa quidditate et non pro aliquo alio subiecto vel denominato ab illa quidditate; sed in ista 'Deus est sapientia,' supponit sapientia pro ipsa deitate quae non est subiectum" (OTh II, 419).

All that Ockham did was to assemble an aggregate of human concepts and then project this aggregate beyond its various human subjects and say, "This stands for God." Whether God is really like that it is simply impossible to tell.

It is no wonder, then, that he finds the triple way of ascending to a knowledge of God of little value. St. Thomas in discussing the *triplex via affirmationis et negationis et eminentiae*—had said that in the negation was contained something positive; that, while we never understood what God was in Himself, by denying of Him certain imperfections we were really affirming other positive perfections.[36] In the *Summa Theologiae*[37] Aquinas states that the perfections we assert of God have a positive signification, that they are, in fact, predicated of God more perfectly than of creatures, at least insofar as what is signified is concerned. Ockham found this unacceptable. Such predication would then have something strictly proper about it. This for him meant an intuition of God as He is in Himself. Consequently he rejected it. He refers to the *triplex via* in the *Sentences* where he is talking about the relationship existing between words, concepts, and things. Words are referred to things through the mediation of concepts. Insofar, then, as something can be understood by us, it can be signified and named by us. Now, God cannot be known in this life according to His essence. But some say that He can be known from creatures insofar as He is their cause, has more perfection than they have, and is without their imperfection.[38] And so God can be known and named from creatures and by creatures. This is a real knowledge, and yet the names signifying God do not express the divine essence as it is in itself. Ockham fails to see where there is any real knowledge involved. In fact, he goes on to say that the whole process does not tell us anything at all. For we might just as well say that God is an angel, since He is the cause of an angel, more perfect than an angel, and not an angel. It is enough to say that we can impose names on God

---

[36]*SCG*, I, c. 4.

[37]*S.Th.* I, q. 13, a. 3; q. 12.

[38]Cf. footnote #33. Ockham, *Scriptum in III Sent.*, q. 9 (OTh VI, 276).

because we can form a concept of Him which can be applied only to Him and that this concept is, therefore, distinct from all other concepts. Where this is possible, a name can be found to signify that particular concept.

To this extent, then, can the human intellect go in its attempt to know God. We are speaking here of the intellect unaided by faith and grace. In that higher order man can know with certainty the many things that God has revealed about Himself. But in the realm of reason and philosophical speculation the knowledge that the human mind can assemble of the divinity is precious little. Philosophically speaking Ockham could grant no more. He had taken his stand on univocity and the cognition of the singular. Having thus limited knowledge of the real order to what was given in actual experience, he could come to no demonstratively certain conclusions which went beyond that order. He can hardly be called a sceptic, since he held as certain many of the conclusions he claimed were undemonstrable. But certainly the seeds of a philosophical agnosticism are there. They would thrive and come to full flower during the centuries which followed.

This becomes increasingly apparent when Ockham deals with the existence of suprasensible realities. All knowledge of existence is had by intuition; and intuition is limited to concrete, singular, existing sensibles. For Ockham abstraction means a precision from existence. Hence all knowledge of anything which is not a sensible existent is necessarily abstract knowledge. As a result, a division is set up between that which is purely intelligible and that which is sensibly existing. The farther, therefore, that one progresses into the realm of the purely intelligible, the farther one gets away from existence. And since these intelligibles can never be verified in the world of experience, they can never be intuited. Ultimately this means that their existential reality can never be verified. Hence the certitude of many conclusions in metaphysics and natural theology is a certitude more properly derived from faith than from reason.

IV
The Divine Ideas

ckham certainly must have been convinced that he had succeeded in establishing the Divine Freedom with regard to the created universe. That universe of singular existents with no necessary connections between them opened it to the causal activity of God at every point. Even granted that the *potentia Dei ordinata* had willed a certain order that was to be followed in the created process, that order was imposed on it by a divinely free will which could still be interrupted or changed by the *potentia Dei absoluta.*

Furthermore he had limited the human intellect to its proper object, the created universe, and had refused to allow any demonstrative knowledge beyond that object. He never denied, of course, that there was more to reality, but to subject a transcendent reality to the laws of logic and human reasoning was further than he was willing to go. After all, what one knew of the transcendent was only what God Himself had revealed of it or what the order of material things could suggest. That order was a finite expression of what God had chosen to do. Behind it lay an Infinite Being Who could have manifested something of Himself in an infinite variety of ways. That Being in Itself was unreachable and unknowable.

Ockham had one more step to take. If he had freed God from any determined way of acting imposed on Him by His own creation, he still had to free God from any determinism imposed on Him by His own nature.

This meant he had to question the doctrine of the Divine Ideas, at least as it was previously understood. And here he had to go very carefully. Hence, we find him beginning with a statement in support of Augustine's position. The Divine Ideas are exemplars toward which the Divine intellect looks in its creative activity.

> I say then that ideas are to be posited precisely as exemplars at which the divine intellect looks in producing creatures. The reason for this is, as the blessed Augustine has said, such ideas are necessary because God acts according to reason. Hence Augustine adds, who would dare to say that God had created irrationally, as if for rational activity there were required only the productive and operative powers and not also the exemplar which provided the pattern for the operation. Now the ideas are not a productive power nor the cause of operation; therefore, they are exemplars.[1]

But while Ockham is willing to state that Ideas are exemplars, he is unwilling to admit that they possess any sort of reality within the Divine Essence. His point of immediate confrontation is with the opinion of Godfrey de Fontibus who held that the Ideas, just as the Divine attributes, differ only by a distinction of reason from the Divine Essence. According to Godfrey—and in somewhat different ways for Aquinas and Scotus—the Ideas are the Divine Essence as imitable outside itself. Just as creatures

---

[1]Ockham, *Scriptum in I Sent.*, d. 35, q. 5: "Ideo dico quod ideae sunt ponendae praecise ut sint exemplaria quaedam ad quae intellectus divinus aspiciens producat creaturas. Cujus ratio est quia, secundum beatum Augustinum ubi supra, propter hoc praecise ponendae sunt ideae in Deo, quia Deus est rationabiliter operans. Unde dicit beatus Augustinus: 'Quis audeat dicere Deum omnis irrationabiliter condidisse?' quasi dicat nullus. Sed ad rationabiliter operandum non requiritur nisi virtus productiva et operativa, et exemplar ad quod aspiciat in operando, et ideae non sunt ipsa virtus productiva vel causativa producentis. Igitur sunt ipsa exemplaria, et ita ut sint exemplaria sunt ponendae" (OTh IV, 492). Cf. also, *Scriptum in I Sent.*, d. 2, q. 2: "Quando aliqua distinguuntur solum per respectus ad extra, impossibile est intelligere illa sine illis extra ... sed potest intelligi quod Deus sit sapiens sine sapientia creaturae; igitur etc." (OTh II, 60).

differ really and in varying degrees from each other, so the Ideas can be rationally distinguished from the Divine Essence and from each other. Ockham's reply is that such a distinction is impossible.

> When some things are distinguished only with relation to something extrinsic, it is impossible to understand them without that extrinsic reference.... But it is quite possible to understand that God is wise without referring to any created wisdom.[2]

Furthermore, such a distinction, whether it be called rational or formal, would still threaten the absolute unity of God. For the Ideas are many and cannot be maintained along with the divine unity. Nor is it possible for the divine knowledge to be dependent in any way either on some realities rationally distinct from itself, or on creatures, whether they be real or only *entia rationis.* The first explanation would reintroduce a Platonic intellectualistic determinism into creation, while the second is simply not tenable in a Christian theology. A further difficulty with the Ideas is that they posit an intelligible pre-existence of the creature. How, then, could creation be said to be *ex nihilo sui et subjecti*?

Now to hold with Augustine that there are Ideas and at the same time refuse to identify them in any way with the divine essence left Ockham only one alternative. He had to identify them in some way with creatures. If, he says, the Ideas are defined in the traditional way as a causative intellectual principle which the agent looks to in producing something in the real order, then the Ideas have no place in the divine essence. The Ideas, then, can only be identified with the creatures.

> The idea is something known by an efficient principle toward which that principle looks in producing something in the real

---

[2]Ockham, *Scriptum in I Sent.,* d. 2, q. 2: "Quando aliqua distinguuntur solum per respectus ad extra, impossibile est intelligere illa sine illis extra...sed potest intelligi quod Deus sit sapiens sine sapientia creaturae; igitur, etc." (OTh II, 60).

order. I say that that description will not apply to the divine essence nor to any sort of relation of reason, but to the creature itself.[3]

The idea of a creature in God can only be the creature itself known directly, perfectly, and individually by God.

> The ideas are not in God subjectively and really but they are in Him only objectively as certain things known by Him, because the ideas are the things themselves as producible by God.... . Furthermore, the ideas are only of singulars and not of species because singulars are precisely what are knowable [4]

Again, if the Idea is not a *ratio cognoscendi,* nor identifiable in any way with the divine knowledge or the divine essence, but predicable only of the creature, what is its ultimate nature? The reply is quite clear. The Ideas are connotative terms or concepts. The mistake has been to make them *quid rei,* something real. Their function is to signify the creature directly and indirectly its producibility by God.[5] This notion is clearly expressed when Ockham deals with the divine attributes.

> Secondly I say that attributable perfections are only certain concepts or signs which are able to be predicated of God, and more appropriately they should be called attributable concepts or names than attributable perfections, because properly speak-

---

[3]Ockham, *Scriptum in I Sent.,* d. 35, q. 5: "Idea est aliquid cognitum a principio effectivo intellectuali ad quod activum aspiciens potest aliquid in esse reali producere. Dico quod ista descriptio non convenit essentiae, nec alicui respectui rationis sed ipsimet creaturae" (OTh IV, 487).

[4]Ockham, *Scriptum in I Sent.,* d. 35, q. 5: "Ideae non sunt in Deo realiter et subjective, sed tantum objective, sicut omnes creaturae ab aeterno fuerunt in Deo quia de aeterno fuerunt cognitae a Deo.... Ideae sunt primo singularium et non specierum quia praecise singularia sunt scibilia" (OTh IV, 497).

[5]Ockham, *Scriptum in I Sent.,* d. 35, q. 5: "Idea importat ipsammet creaturam in recto et etiam ipsammet in obliquo et praeter hoc importat ipsam divinam cognitionem vel cognoscentem in obliquo; et ideo de ipsamet creatura est predicabilis ut ipsa sit idea, sed non est predicabilis de agente cognoscente, quia nec cognitio nec cognoscens est idea, sicut nec examplar" (OTh IV, 497).

ing a perfection is always something and these concepts are not
properly things, nor are they simply perfections.[6]

He then proceeds to clarify further what he means by the divine
attributes. These concepts or names imply or refer to the divine
essence in various ways. Some imply the divine essence absolutely and affirmatively; some only connote the divine essence
by referring to something else; and some are simply negative. Of
the first kind are names like intellect and will. Predestining or
creating would be of the second kind, while incorruptible and
immortal would be examples of the third kind. Only in this way
can we speak of a plurality of attributes predicable of the divine
essence. But they can never be identified in any way with that
essence, since they are only names or concepts.[7] Hence, such
concepts are beings of reason and distinguished from each other
as one concept is from another. They can be predicated of the
divine essence because they stand for it or substitute for it. Again
it is clear that as names or concepts there is no way to identify
them really or formally with the essence itself.

Now, while the Ideas are similar to the attributes, they are not
exactly the same. The Ideas, too, are names or concepts, but they
have different connotations and are not predicable of God in the
same way as are the attributes. For, as has been seen, the Ideas
signify the creature directly and God only obliquely.

> Fourthly I say that ... the ideas are not distinguished in God as
> attributes because the ideas in God are the things themselves

---

[6]Ockham, *Scriptum in I Sent.*, d. 2, q. 1: "Secundo modo dico quod non sunt nisi
quidam conceptus vel signa quae possunt vere predicari de Dei, et magis proprie
deberent dici conceptus attributales vel nomina attributalia quam perfectiones
attributales, quia proprie perfectio non est nisi res aliqua, et tales conceptus non
sunt proprie res, vel non sunt perfectae, quia saltem non sunt perfectiones
simpliciter" (OTh II, 61).

[7]Ockham, *Scriptum in I Sent.*, d. 2, q. 1 (OTh II, 61).

as producible by God. Nor are they predicated of God really as the attributes are truly predicated of God.[8]

Such names or concepts exist only in our intellects, and the only distinction possible is the one made by the intellect. Such distinction can in no way be applied to the divine essence. Understood in this way the Divine Ideas signify not something in God Himself but the creature as creatable. In this way Ockham can agree with Augustine that for every creature real or possible there is a Divine Idea. In God such an Idea is nothing. Hence, it leaves creation free and *ex nihilo* and at the same time does no violence to the divine simplicity or unity. Such Ideas are also eternal, for the created real was eternally producible and all possible creatures insofar as they are truly possible and free from contradiction, are also producible.

Some Consequences of Ockham's Position

Ockham's reinterpretation of the doctrine of Divine Ideas certainly succeeded in establishing a God free from any Greek determinism and in asserting a God Who could freely and really create from nothing. But one can wonder whether the price he had to pay for the position be upheld was worth it. If we look for a moment at the nature of Ockham's finite reality, several things become apparent. That reality is primarily the effect of a creating will. And while it is kept from arbitrariness by reason of that will's identity with the divine intellect, nevertheless it is grounded in free choice and not in any absolute divine intelligibility. Things could always have been otherwise, again granting the principle of non-contradiction.

Now what God wills are singular existents, each of which is independent of all the others. Any connection between them, any ordering of one to another, is the result of that creating will.

---

[8]Ockham, *Scriptum in I Sent.*, d. 2, q. 1: "Ad quartum dico...quod ideae non distinguuntur in Deo sicut attributa quia ideae in Deo sunt ipsae res producibiles a Deo, nec predicantur de Deo sicut ipsa attributa vere de Deo predicantur" (OTh II, 71).

Each is a finite essence, and however temporarily stable such an essence may be, it reflects no necessary intelligibility in the divine essence but only what God has freely chosen to accomplish in this historical order. Further, this historical order of things, since it is neither essentially nor existentially necessary, is subject, not to divine whimsy certainly, but at least to change in all its aspects. The relations between things are consistent enough so that one can talk about normal and abnormal sequence. But there always remains the possibility that such a normal sequence of events may be changed by the *potentia Dei absoluta* and exhibit different and unlooked for manifestations of that higher order. If, for example, each thing and event is singular and distinct in its own right, then why not have the seeing of the star without the star? It is equally possible to have stars without the seeing of them. It is one thing to dispense with Divine Ideas. It is another thing entirely, once one has dispensed with them, to keep creation very stable or grounded in any absolute.

If one takes the position that Ockham's whole approach was based on the divine freedom, that starting point is reflected in his theory of knowledge. One encounters a *de facto* existing singular which speaks only of itself and in a rather unstable fashion at that. All connections between such singulars are also *de facto*, sequential, and just as unstable. It is a universe which the knower can organize according to certain logical patterns, but such patterns remain a way of dealing with things, not with the way things are or even ought to be. It is better, I think, to regard Ockham as a conceptualist rather than as a nominalist, but it is also easy to see why the charge of nominalism has been lodged against him so consistently. In the epistemological order one is forced, beyond the original existential intuition, to deal with things according to a mutual relationship of concepts and terms. The concept may and does reflect the thing, but relationships are much more between the concepts themselves than between the things.

It will follow, too, that there can be few if any arguments based on causality which could transcend such a created order. If all we can know is a finite being which manifests only a very limited aspect of the divine will, and if that Creator, furthermore, had given the power to create to one of His creatures, then there is little hope for any proof for the existence of God from effect to cause, at least to an infinite cause.

All of Ockham's difficulties with a knowledge of God can also be seen as logical consequences of his previously chosen position. Every created effect is not an expression of an intelligibility grounded in the nature of God Himself, but a finite extrapolation of the divine will's power to produce. One can add up and combine finite perfections into a complex concept no longer applicable to any creature, but neither will such a concept give any insight into the divine nature. At best it will stand for, or substitute for, such an unknowable essence. It would seem that the whole previously accepted philosophy of the divine nature is reduced to probable reflections on a concept which is neither finite nor infinite.

There is one further difficulty, and it is an important one: How God can any longer be said to know creatures. Where does the divine intellect terminate? It cannot terminate at the creature as possible, for before it is real, the only real source of possibility is God Himself. Neither can it terminate at the creature as actual, for this would be to put the divine intellect under specification by the creature. It can only be said that the divine intellect terminates in the divine essence itself. But, if there are no ideas of creatures in that essence, then God can only know Himself. In rescuing the unity of God from Platonic ideas Ockham comes perilously close to the God of Aristotle—pure thought thinking only itself. He was surely aware of the difficulty. But he could not simply submit to it and agree that God does not know His creation. But how He does so remains for Ockham a moot question. Perhaps today he would have referred to it as a meaningless question. He insists that God does know all things. The *how* must remain part of that *Mysterium tremendum* which no created intellect can know in this life. It is better in the end to leave God in mystery than to explain His activity in a way which would destroy either His unity or His infinity.

Ex hoc ipso quod Deus est Deus cognoscit omnia.[9]

Ockham, it seems, was willing to accept without question the difficulties his system gave rise to. If these are the natural consequences of a philosophical approach to a free Christian God, so be it. He is almost blasé at times about the inadequacy of philosophical proof. The phrase, *non potest demonstrari*, is a constant refrain when he is dealing with philosophical positions. He seems to take for granted that the philosophical enterprise engaged in with a view to establishing a metaphysics, especially a metaphysics of the Absolute, is at best an unrewarding effort.

Ockham's God is one accepted in faith. And that faith informed him that God freely created the world. His task, he thought, was to maintain and safeguard such a God. He was convinced that with the introduction of the Aristotelian metaphysics his predecessors had failed to do so. Hence, there arose his whole attempt to restore to Christianity its rightful God. He is thoroughly dedicated to the basic Augustinian position formulated in the *"Credo ut intelligam."* What he has been accused of is that he came more and more to restrict the range of the *intelligo* and extend more and more the object of the *credo*.

Conclusion

It is also important to recognize that Ockham for all his philosophical scepticism never surrendered the ability of the human mind to achieve certitude. In the *Summa Logicae,* for example, he writes clearly about the various meanings of *"scire"* and the evident comprehension of necessary truth.[10] But it is in theology grounded in and infused by faith that truly certain conclusions can be arrived at. It is important to note here that the source of the certitude is not the theological process but the faith from which that process flows. The same process followed by an

---

[9]Ockham, *I Sent.*, 35, 5 R. (OTh, 497 ff.).

[10]Ockham, *Summa Logicae,* Pars III-2, c. 1. (OPh I, 506).

unbeliever would arrive at only probable conclusions. For the unbeliever has to assume certain premises and then proceed logically to conclusions derived from them. But the unbeliever's assumption does not make the premises any more certain in themselves. They remain probable, and the best any unbeliever can do is to recognize that the conclusion arrived at would follow certainly, only if the premises had been accepted as certain.

What then distinguishes the theological habit grounded in faith from the probable conclusions of the non-believer? It is the certitude which flows from faith, the firm adherence to premises accepted as revealed, which leads one beyond probability and all fear of error.[11] Quoting Augustine he speaks further about this certitude generated by faith.

> Faith is the presence of things absent; faith is the interior possession of what is external; faith is the internal vision of what is not seen. From Augustine's authority it is clear that, although some things are not intuited but known only abstractively, nevertheless the faith by which they are believed is intuited and not just known abstractively.[12]

This certitude in faith includes both necessary and contingent propositions. This is true since the certitude comes neither from the necessary connection between subject and predicate nor by a deductive process. There is no evidence shining out of the revealed proposition leading to a demonstrative conclusion. Nor are contingent propositions any less capable of being held with certitude; for they, too, as revealed and accepted in faith, probable as they may be in themselves, partake in the certitude provided by faith. It must be noted also that propositions taken from other areas of knowledge may be appropriated by theology, but in this case the guarantee for the truth of the proposition is faith not evidence.

---

[11]Ockham, *Scriptum in I Sent.*, Prol., q. 1. For Ockham's treatment of theology as a science and the certitude of its conclusions, cf. Q. I of the *Prologue* in its entirety. (OTh I, 1).

[12]Ockham, *Scriptum in I Sent.*, Prol. q. 1 (OTh I, 41).

Ockham was still not finished. He had separated demonstrative knowledge from faith. But he had not separated faith from certitude. And on his own terms he was willing to reunite them. There can be no faith in demonstrative or evident knowledge. But, on the other hand, theology can open itself to all areas of knowledge, elevate those areas to a certitude which they could never have of themselves. In a sense, all natural knowledge is assumed by theology, clarified by it, and related to an end far beyond the natural one. Hence, all other areas of knowledge become in truth the handmaidens of theology. As G. Leff writes:

> Ockham's uncompromising refusal to allow theology any dependence upon evident knowledge shows a Christian awareness as great as any of the scholastics and a rigour greater than all of them: he repeatedly reduces previous attempts to establish a bridge between theology and knowledge by the argument that theology would then be open to the unbeliever and the believer alike. This does not however lead him to reduce theology to a mere act of belief. Which brings us to the second conclusion: that if on the one hand faith makes theology inaccessible to natural knowledge, on the other hand it makes natural knowledge accessible to theology... . Theology can therefore draw upon all the other sciences and every kind of knowledge, necessary, contingent, complex, incomplex to increase faith, just because assent to all theological truth is from preexisting faith.[13]

It is here finally in theology that whatever is doubtful or uncertain on the purely natural level—and especially in many of the conclusions of the metaphysicians—is given a surety and a certitude which go beyond all natural certitude or the lack thereof. In a world of limited insight and limited evidence, a world freely created by a God Who may have manifested something of His *potentia ordinata*, but Whose *potentia absoluta* is infinite, Ockham can well afford to doubt many a metaphysical conclusion. What he could never doubt were propositions flowing out of faith, even when they repeated the same doubtful conclusions drawn from the merely natural order of things. He

---

[13]Leff, G., *William of Ockham*, (Manchester University Press, Rowman and Littlefield, 1975), pp. 358-59.

was aware certainly of the distinction some of his predecessors had made between an order of natural truth achievable by human reason and an order of strictly supernatural truth accessible only through faith. Nor did he ever deny that human reason could naturally acquire truth. But it was a limited truth restricted to an empirical base. And the range of the human intellect was limited for its certitude to that order. The intellect could speculate about non-empirical truths, but the conclusions reached were probable, based on persuasive reasons.

That sort of limit placed on the human intellect was, it seems, the price Ockham had to pay for the divine freedom he was so eager to establish. The world and man were the way God had freely created them. Both were manifestations only of a *de facto* order freely established in which God could still operate, if He chose. Again, short of contradiction, God could change the present order of things. The Divine Will assumes a pre-eminence here which leaves the Divine Intelligibility shrouded in mystery. Now if that mysterious God chose to manifest to man another order of truth beyond the capability of human resource and guarantee it with His own truth, then we could only be grateful for the gift and accept the certitude which went with it. At this point there is a fusion of the natural and the supernatural with the higher truth elevating all purely natural truth and infusing it with a certitude it could not have of itself.

Part of the difficulty in interpreting Ockham may well be in the attempt of historians of philosophy to base their judgments of his work solely on his logic, epistemology, and metaphysics. One can talk of a Thomistic metaphysics or of a Scotistic epistemology much more readily than one can talk of an Ockhamistic philosophy. The distinction between philosophy and theology tends to fade out in Ockham, or, better, philosophy tends to become much more subordinate to theology. In this he is more Augustinian despite his knowledge of Aristotle. Ockham is predominantly a theologian and shapes his philosophical position to fit that theological purpose.

Furthermore, if it be granted that the theological end in view was primarily to establish the creative freedom of the God of Christianity, then it becomes more understandable why he had to revise previous metaphysical and epistemological approaches to put the divine freedom beyond question. It is true that in doing so he raised serious questions about the extent and validity of the exercise of the human intellect. It is also true that, if one subtracts the certitude engendered by faith, his philosophical system seems to open the way to scepticism. Ockham, perhaps, would not have been seriously concerned. Such a separation would not have occurred to him as meaningful. Neither did it seem so to Augustine. And in the long run, despite his clear reliance on Aristotle in many areas, he remains well within his Franciscan and Augustinian tradition.

V
The Via Moderna

f the preceding interpretation of Ockham's basic position is correct, namely his attempt to establish the divine freedom which Christianity demanded, the emphasis changed in the centuries which followed. Ockham, as we have seen, thought it necessary to modify radically many of the positions held by his predecessors. These included a much more restricted theory of knowledge, a radical change in the nature of causality with its corresponding limitation of the possibility of demonstrative proof, an insistence on the omnipotence of God, and a transference to the realm of faith of many propositions previously accepted as provable by human reason. Ockham had opened a new way, and there were many who eagerly followed it. It should be noted, however, that the new movement could hardly be called Ockhamist in a univocal sense. Even those who are so designated exhibit a great variety in their theological and philosophical thinking and are not infrequently opposed to one another.

There are, however general trends which are characteristic and which engage the interest of those who committed themselves to the *Via Moderna*. There is the distinction between intuitive and abstract knowledge and the development of a logic based on abstract knowledge with its attendant conceptualism and its concentration on terms and their mutual relationships in a proposition. "Universality" is treated in a purely functional way indicating not any common nature shared by many singulars but simply as a sign standing for many. Hence a theory of "supposition" had to be developed—the way in which terms and concepts can signify things.

The above obviously presupposed the acceptance of Ockham's world of unique singulars together with the rejection of anything like a real distinction between essence and existence or even between substance and accidents. Causality in such a world could only mean habitual association and sequence. An interesting conflict in this regard arose over the nature of motion. Ockham had denied the existence of motion as a separate entity from the moving body. He held that motion was merely a term replacing a series of statements that the body was here, now there, and so forth. Others such as John Buridan, Albert of Saxony, and Nicholas of Oresme were not only convinced of the reality of motion but, through their attempts to discover its proper cause, contributed to the origin of modern science.

The theory of divine omnipotence based on what God could will without contradiction remained a dominant theme. Instead of a universe conceived as an expression of divine intelligibility, there is posited a universe radically contingent upon the divine will, even to the natures of things themselves. This same notion appears in ethics and morality, in which sin comes to be equated with prohibition and good is determined by the will of God and not by any intrinsic principle found in the objects of choice. Many of the Ockhamists went so far as to assert that God could command someone to hate Him and that obeying such a command would be meritorious. This seems less strange, if good and evil are determined only by what God wills them to be.

There is found, too, an increasing importance for the role of faith. The restriction of demonstrative knowledge to arguments proceeding from empirical data produced an ever widening gap between philosophy and theology. Granted the Ockhamistic approach to metaphysics and logic, philosophy became more and more a study of the material world and a quasi science of predictability about events in nature and a corresponding scepticism about anything beyond.

Some Important Names

The main themes of the new movement appear consistently in the works of such men as Robert Holcot, Adam Wodam, Gregory of Rimini, Peter of Ailly, and Ockham's commentator, Gabriel Biel. The two men who best represent the extremes of the position are John of Mirecourt and Nicholas of Autrecourt. John of Mirecourt divides all knowledge into that which is evident and that which is held with fear of error. Evident knowledge in the strictest sense is that which can be reduced to the principle of contradiction. Experiential knowledge is also evident, but it is never capable of leading to a strict demonstration. The proofs for God's existence and the causal proposition are classed under the knowledge that is held with fear of error. The theme of the divine omnipotence also shows up strongly. God can cause any act and that act will be good, even if it should be contrary to the natural law.

Nicholas of Autrecourt held also that the only certain knowledge was that which could be reduced to the principle of contradiction. Experience provides certain knowledge, but in a universe of individuals the existence of one thing can never be inferred from the existence of another. It is impossible for logic to detect any necessary connections in nature. In his philosophy of nature Nicholas returned to the old Greek atomism, preferring it to the hylomorphic theory of Aristotle. Such a universe of disparate atoms was all the more dependent on God.

An indication of how far the position of Nicholas had progressed to an almost total empiricism can be seen from several propositions condemned by Pope Clement VI in 1346.

11. That with the exception of the certitude coming from faith there is no other certitude unless it be that of the first principle and what can be resolved into it.

14. That it is not evident that any other thing besides God can be the cause of any effect—that any other cause except God can be an efficient cause—or that there can be any natural efficient cause.

30. That the following conclusions are not evident: There is an act of understanding; therefore there is an intellect. There is an act of willing; therefore there is a will.

53. That this is the first principle and there is no other: "if something is, something is."[1]

It is further, perhaps, than Ockham would have been willing to go. On the other hand, as Gilson points out,[2] a sure way to protect the faith against philosophical attacks by Averroists and others was to prove that philosophy could not prove anything. This effectively took theology out of the hands of the philosophers. It also deprived theology of any philosophical support. Ockham himself had been content to say that theology was not a science and that its certitude came not from reason but from faith.

The *Via Moderna* and Religion

There were two quite predictable reactions to the position outlined above. The one was on the part of the so-called speculative mystics and the other on the part of those who accepted the criticism of philosophy, who were also disenchanted with the endless bickering of the theologians, and who opted for a more practical and simpler way.

Among the speculative mystics are included men like Meister Eckhart (1260 - 1327), John Tauler (1300 - 1361), Blessed Henry Suso (1295 - 1366), and John Ruysbroeck (1293 - 1381). In general their approach led them back, at least to some extent, to Aquinas, Bonaventure, the Pseudo-Dionysius, and Augustine. If God could not be found either in nature or in demonstration, then one must turn inward where He manifested Himself in the *scintilla animae*, the noblest part of the soul. It is here that He

---

[1] *Enchiridion Symbolorum*, Denziger, H., ed. by Carl Rahner, S.J., Herder, Freiburg in Breisgau, 1955, p. 234 ff. (Translation my own.)

[2] Gilson, E., *The Unity of Philosophical Experience*, NY, Charles Scribner's Sons, 1937, pp. 97 ff.

could be approached as Pure Understanding, Absolute Existence, or the Good and the True. And it is here also that God disappears from all attempts of human reason to grasp Him. One can speak of the Cloud of Unknowing, the Darkness beyond all being and knowledge, or in Eckhart's phrase: *Die Wüsste Gottheit*—the wilderness of the Godhead. Man is drawn to that infinite and unknowable wilderness by the scintilla within him, the divine spark that makes him an image of God, and which draws him inexorably toward that unknown God.

It is an approach to God which simply by-passes and transcends the logical difficulties and objections concerned with demonstrative knowledge and turns toward a God Who is beyond all knowledge because He dwells in inaccessible darkness. At this point one needs neither philosophy nor theology. And one can permit the followers of Ockham and the *Via Moderna* to play their own games on their own turf. What after all had Christian Platonism to do with Aristotle?

The second reaction to the theologians and the logicians was an attempt to have done with all the disputations of the various schools and return to the Gospels and the way of life which would insure the salvation of one's soul. In his letter to the Colossians St. Paul had warned against the deceit and vanity to which philosophy can lead. And as far back as the secondary century Tertullian had asked what Jerusalem had to do with Athens, or what sort of relation could there ever be between the Church and the Academy. Now in the fourteenth century the same cry was again raised. What had Paris to do with Assisi or Plato and Aristotle with the Fathers of the Church. Piety and not speculation, prayer and penance and not logic or metaphysics, the imitation of Christ and not the theologians—these would lead to man's true and only real goal, the salvation of his immortal soul. Such was the position taken by Gehrard Groot, who also established a way of putting into practice what he preached by founding the Brothers of the Common Life whose guiding ideal was the contempt of the world and the imitation of the humble life of Christ. One of his best known successors was Thomas a Kempis, the probable author of *The Imitation of Christ*. As E. Gilson has remarked: "... anyone who remembers the three opening chapters of *The Imitation of Christ* can consider himself fully informed about the fourteenth century anti-scholasticism."[3]

Jean Gerson (1363-1429)

One of the leading proponents of practical mystical theology, Jean Gerson, became chancellor of the University of Paris at an early age. He was a theologian in his own right and like Ockham an opponent of Scotistic formalism and all attempts to question in any way the Divine Freedom. Hence he rejected the doctrine of the divine ideas, regarding it as an attack on the unity of God and a subjection of the free divine will to an intellectual determinism reminiscent of Plato himself. Like Ockham he insisted on the divine will as the ultimate source of both meaning and being and it was from this viewpoint that he rejected the new Averroism and the return to what he considered the Platonism of Scotus and the "Formalizantes." Because of this he was accepted and welcomed by the Ockhamists and Nominalists of his time as one of their own.

Although Gerson's nominalism has been seriously questioned by A. Combes and at least modified by F. Copleston, there seems to be enough of it in his writings to use him as an example of its historical development. Gerson's best known work is his treatise on speculative and practical mystical theology.[4] In several instances in this work the influence of Ockham is quite evident. These are very important instances because Gerson uses an Ockhamistic epistemology to explain how the position he takes is justifiable.

Mysticism had always been recognized as a valid approach to God. It had also been acknowledged that the mystic's way included the affections and the emotions, which were generally

---

[3]*Ibid.*, pp. 94-95.

[4]A. Combes, ed., *Joannes Carlerii de Gerson de Mistica Theologia* (Lugano: Thesaurus Mundi, 1958).

absent from the more intellectualistic approach of the speculative theologians, at least in the fourteenth century. There is, of
course, an affective element in Augustine and Bonaventure, but
they never excluded either reason or insight. The case, however,
is quite different with someone like Gerson. If, like Ockham, he
allows no real knowledge of God but is left with a formulated
concept taken from things, then the problem becomes obvious.
What does the mystic deal with? What sort of knowledge does he
achieve? And, more practically, what does he love and what does
he serve? Let us follow Gerson, as he attempts to answer the
questions.

Gerson turned to mystical theology as an antidote to the confusion, the scepticism, and the logic chopping of the speculative
theologians of the time. Mystical theology, he tells us, is the
most certain of all and almost entirely free from the dissensions
of the schools. It is grounded immediately in internal experience, and there is nothing more certain than this. The knowledge
of its principles is had through faith, than which, again, nothing
is more certain. This grounding in internal experience is quite
different from all other types of knowledge, including that of
philosophy and speculative theology which take their origin
from external experience.[5]

After treating of the soul, its nature, and its powers in the usual
scholastic fashion, Gerson continues to contrast mystical theology with the speculative theology taught in the schools. In the
first place, mystical theology is better acquired through affective
penance than through intellectual investigation. This indicates
its superiority, since it is clear that love is superior to knowledge,
the will to the intellect, and charity to faith. Hence, he can define
mystical theology as the reaching out of the soul to God through
the desire of love. He takes another definition from the Pseudo-
Dionysius, according to whom mystical theology is irrational
and non-intellectual; it is foolish wisdom exceeding all praise:

> Mystical theology is a striving of the soul for God through the
> desire of love.

---

[5]*Ibid.*, p. 70.

> Mystical theology is an experimental knowledge of God through
> the embrace of unitive love.
>
> Or, as Dionysius said: "Mystical theology is irrational and
> delirious; it is stupid wisdom exceeding all praise."[6]

Still further distinctions between speculative and mystical theology can be made. The former is located in the intellectual
potency of the soul; the latter, in the affective. The object of the
first is truth; that of the second, good. Speculative theology
makes use of philosophy, of rigid and subtle concepts and
methods. Mystical theology needs no such tools. It concentrates
rather on the affections and the practice of the moral virtues. For
this reason anyone can achieve the most perfect certitude from
mystical theology, which is not true of the speculative. There is
much more, but the general tenor is the same. Love is better than
knowledge, the exercise of virtue and pious affection superior to
intellectual insight, union with God more perfect than learned
disquisition about him.

This has always been a traditional view among Christian writers
and not an untenable one. But previously knowledge had always
been considered, if not the primary, at least an essential element
in the process. If Ockham is correct, however, and our intellects
can provide us with very little knowledge of God, it becomes
easier for Gerson to minimize knowledge as an element in
mystical theology. This is especially true when one of the rules
for success in the mystical approach is precisely the suppression
of phantasms and images upon which all knowledge is based.

Now the question arises: How is it possible to suppress images?
And, secondly, once these are suppressed, How is it possible to
ascend to God independently of any knowledge of him? Gerson
attacks the problem in a short work appended to the *De Mystica
Theologia*. It is entitled *Elucidatio Scholastica Theologiae*

---

[6]*Ibid.*, pp. 70 ff. "Theologia mistica est extensio animi in Deum per amoris
desiderium. Theologia mistica est cognitio experimentalis habita de Deo per
amoris unitivi complexum vel sic per Dionysium: theologia mistica est irrationalis
et amens, et stulta sapientia, excedens laudantes."

Mysticae.[7] He begins by quoting St. Paul, Dionysius, and Hugo de Palma, all of whom testify to an ecstatic love of God *"absque previa vel concomitante cognitione."*[8] This love without knowledge can take place in three ways. It can be a purely natural love, it can be entirely supernatural, and it can also be an habitual love. Intellectual cognition is also threefold: direct, reflexive, and a simple or complex variation of each.[9]

There are examples of beings driven by love toward their goals, and yet these beings do not possess any knowledge. The heavens strive for a goal imposed on them by God without any knowledge of what that goal may be:

> There is no knowledge in the material heavens, nor in anything else lacking a soul; but in virtue of a love impressed on them by the first intelligence they are moved unerringly toward their goal more certainly than an arrow is moved toward its target by the archer.[10]

There is the same natural finality in man who, without even knowing it, is driven toward God! "It is clear that man is moved toward God by a non-free natural love, not from some natural knowledge in him which would cause such a love."[11]

And it is doubtful whether there can be any cognoscitive potency which is not also appetitive. There can be no being which does not seek the good. But, as has been said above, the reverse is not

---

[7]Cf. n. 4 above.

[8]*Elucidatio Scholastica Theologiae Misticae*, p. 221.

[9]*Ibid.*, p. 223.

[10]*Ibid.* "Non est autem in celo materiali, sicut nec in rebus aliis anima carentibus, cognitio, quamvis pondere sui amoris impresso ab intelligentia prima non errante feruntur quo feruntur, multo verius et certius quam sagitta moveatur ad signum ex impetu per sagittantem impresso."

[11]*Ibid.*, p. 224. "Stat hominem per amorem naturalem non liberum ferri in Deum, non ex actuali cognitione, quae talem in ipso causet amorem."

true. There are appetitive beings without knowledge. It is easier when we consider mysticism as an infused grace. If what Gerson had previously said about knowledge was commonly accepted by mystical theologians, here his debt to Ockham is manifest. On this level it is clear that God could give and conserve a free act of love in a person after the act of knowledge which gave rise to it has been destroyed. And if this is true, there is no reason to think that God could not produce an act of love without any previous act of knowledge:

> It is clear that man is moved toward God by a free love supernaturally infused or conserved without any prior or concurrent free knowledge with respect to that love.

> It is also clear that God could conserve an act of love freely elicited from man after the act of knowledge accompanying it has been destroyed.

> Granted this, a man would then love God without intellectually knowing Him, at least with an elicited act of knowledge.[12]

This is reminiscent not only of the Ockhamistic distinction between the *"potentia Dei absoluta"* and the *"potentia Dei ordinata,"* but also of the equally Ockhamistic notion of the absolute individuality of the difference between entities. Just as the seeing of a star can be produced by God without a star being present, so, too, can God produce an act of loving independently of any act of knowing. The position is further strengthened by the realization that no natural act of knowledge could possibly be the cause of such an act of love, which is purely Christian and which in its experimental affectiveness has nothing to do with apprehension and judgment.

Yet one must go cautiously here. In the tradition of mystical theology there are others who speak of a love independent of

---

[12]*Ibid.*, p. 225. "Stat hominem ferri in Deum per amorem liberum supernaturaliter infusum vel conservatum, nulla in ipso cognitione libera comitante vel previa respectu illius amoris.

Constat enim quod amorem libere elicitum ab homine posset Deus conservare, destructo omnis cognitionis actu; quo posito, diligeret homo Deum tunc intellectualiter non cognitum, saltem cognitione que est actus secundus elicitus."

knowledge. In the *Summa Theologiae*, for example, Aquinas speaks of a natural love by which both angels and men and all creatures are inclined to God more than they are to themselves.[13] In response to the fourth objection in the same article, he states quite clearly, "It must be said that God, in so far as He is the universal good, from which depends every natural good, is loved with a natural love by each one."[14]

And in the *Prima Secundae*, where he is treating of the cause of love, Aquinas, while holding the position that there is no love without knowledge, is willing to qualify it somewhat. In dealing with the objection from Dionysius he admits that the love of the end is in all things, whether they have knowledge or not. He does add, however, that the knowledge responsible for such love is in God who created such natures: "It must be said that natural love also, which is in all things, is caused by some knowledge. This knowledge may not be in the natural things themselves, but in Him who instituted the natural order...."[15] Again later on he speaks of a love of God which is connatural to man and even to non-knowing creatures according to the mode proper to each.[16]

A contemporary theologian, Bernard Lonergan, who is certainly no Ockhamist, is quite willing to admit, at least in one case, the primacy of love over knowledge. He writes as follows:

> It used to be said, *Nihil amatum nisi praecognitum*, Knowledge precedes love.... But the major exception to the Latin tag is God's gift of his love flooding our hearts. Then we are in the dynamic state of being in love. But who it is we love, is neither given nor as yet understood. Our capacity for moral self-transcendence has found a fulfillment that brings deep joy and profound peace. Our love reveals to us values we had not appreciated, values of prayer and worship, or repentance and

---

[13]*Summa Theologiae*, I, 60, 5.

[14]*Ibid.*, ad 4.

[15]*Ibid.*, I-II, 27, 2 ad 3.

[16]*Ibid.*, I-II, 109, 3.

belief. But if we would know what is going on within us, if we would learn to integrate it with the rest of our living, we have to inquire, investigate, seek counsel. So it is that in religious matters love precedes knowledge and, as that love is God's gift, the very beginning of faith is due to God's grace.[17]

If this is what Gerson is saying, then it is only fair to admit that the Ockhamistic interpretation given above certainly can be questioned.

Practically too, Gerson is a bit more cautious. For it does seem to be clear that some sort of actual knowledge accompanies such infused love because the soul judges that it loves and is aware of taking delight in God. But this is an experiential awareness of a condition of the soul and not of its object. Or, rather, the object is this condition of the soul and not God. It is this awareness which the mystical theologian writes about when he attempts to describe what happens. Hence, one can agree with the traditional teaching of the philosophers and theologians that there is no love without some knowledge. On the other hand, the knowledge involved need not be a reflexive knowledge, and much less need it be discursive or intuitive. That is why the mystical approach to God is open to the educated and the uneducated alike.

It seems to me that what Gerson has done has been to justify theoretically an approach to God which need not involve a cognitive element. It is the perfect answer to the charge that one cannot get to God because no one can know what God is like. The reply is simple: knowledge is not necessary. It is true that he modifies his stand in the face of actual experience and practice. But so did Ockham, when he agreed that God could create the seeing of a star without there being an actual star to see, by stating that this is not the ordinary way things happen. It may not be the ordinary way God operates, but it is certainly within his *"potentia absoluta."*

---

[17]Lonergan, *Method in Theology* (NY: Herder and Herder, 1972), p. 122.

I tend to agree with F. Copleston that it would be a mistake to look upon Gerson as a convinced Ockhamist struggling to be a mystic. But there are certainly Ockhamistic assumptions in his writings. On the other hand, there is not the total rejection of an intellectual insight into any reality that transcends the material singular, as there is in Ockham. But it also is true that what Gerson grants a knowledge of is not God but rather the effect produced by God in the soul and will and affections of the individual. Perhaps Gerson was led to moderate his position somewhat by his own personal experience that love can and does provide a kind of knowledge, however weak that knowledge may be, of the immaterial. At least he quotes Augustine to the effect that we can love the unseen, but never the unknown.

The mystical approach grew in popularity as the century progressed. There is more and more concern with a negative theology which can be seen in a highly sophisticated state in Nicholas of Cusa's *De Docta Ignorantia*. But the new approach had its dark side also. Gerson consistently inveighs against a false mysticism, pseudo-private revelations, superstition, and outright fakery and nonsense. This does not mean to suggest that this darker side is in any way peculiar to the fourteenth century.
Perhaps one of the lessons that Gerson can teach us is that there is in man an ordination to the Divine. To block one such road is simply to drive the creature along another. If the way of knowledge is narrowed and even closed, then there is the way of the will and the affections. Scepticism may replace proof, but faith and belief can take up the slack. Experience of the immediate world may hem us in, but man still feels the call of the Transcendent. And it seems he will seek it one way or another.

The danger is that one really will worship an unknown God, and that he will do so on a level from which reason and knowledge have been exiled. It is clear since David Hume what has happened to one whole area of philosophy. Not only did Hume lose God, but eventually he also lost the world and had to settle for a personal experience of himself. The same danger is there for contemporary man. It has become evident that in the twentieth just as in the fourteenth century, system and demonstration are not enough. Twentieth century man is just as intellectually disillusioned as was his fourteenth century counterpart. He seems to be overpowered by a scepticism and a world which only science still seems to be able to deal with on a rational level. But science is considered for the most part to have joined hands with materialism. What is to become of the individual who clings to belief in the Transcendent and wants to make contact somehow? The desire and the will to do so are still there. If the Spirit no longer speaks wisdom, he can and may speak to the heart and the affections. Gerson would approve and feel at home in our century.

There is, however, a difference. Gerson used mystical theology not only as an escape from scepticism but as a way of experiencing what went on in the soul of one who sought God. What was experienced was some sort of an affective, voluntary reaction of the self to a God that faith assured one was real. In this respect the soul was drawn out of itself to rest, if not in God himself, at least in the certitude that revelation and the truths of faith were still operative. The process may be less objective than that today.

It is not difficult to get the impression that some contemporary approaches to God are not very much interested in certitude or in finding in revelation and love a direction for the soul to go out of itself that it may cling to an objective, transcendent God, who is also transcendent Being. On the contrary, there seems to be an attempt to turn the human person within himself and to use theology, revelation, and even God as an emotional and psychological support against the confusion and meaninglessness that haunt the modern world. The need to "get-it-all-together," to find personal peace, to achieve emotional maturity may become the primary goal in view as opposed to the only real goal, which is God. In other words, what faith, love, revelation, and affective Christianity do for the individual himself become more important than the source and object of all these. At this point, I think, the chancellor would stick. The practice of mystical theology was meant to lead to God and nowhere else. If the practitioner were aided in the process to acquire a deeper faith, love, and certitude—and this would certainly happen—this was all to the good. But for Gerson the goal was always God and never the self.

As a matter of fact, it is only by withdrawing from the self that the process has any chance at all of success. In this he is closer to the thirteenth century than to the twentieth.

VI
Conclusion

t is always difficult, if not impossible, to sum-
marize the work of any philosopher, espe-
cially when that work touches most areas of
philosophy and theology. William of Ockham
is no exception. However, there are some basic
themes which run through his writings and
which have been historically recognized as
characteristic of his thought. The first of these is the complete
individuality of all existing things. This is not particularly new
or unique. No one really since Plato had taught that universals
existed as such. But Scotus, for example, had proposed a realism
which found in existing things themselves formalities which
corresponded to our concepts and which could be conceptually
isolated. These formal intelligibilities in the things were not
really distinct and yet more than simply different aspects under
which the intellect could approach the thing. It was against such
formal complexity that Ockham reacted, insisting on the complete individuality of any and all existents and reserving such
formal distinctions to the conceptual order. Thought could deal
with the world in a variety of ways once it got beyond the
intuition of the singular. But that variety indicated only an
attempt on the part of the intellect to understand what was in
itself a unique existent.

In the second place Ockham saw these existents as radically
dependent on a cause, be it God or something else. Again, this is
not new or startling. All previous medieval philosophers would
willingly agree. But Ockham went further. Not only did he insist
on existential contingency, but, in accord with his stress on

divine omnipotence, on essential contingency as well. Things were dependent on the will of God for their being and also for being what they were. There were no necessary intelligibilities or laws of pure reason which God had to respect in creating a man, or an animal, or a plant-always granting, of course, the principle of non-contradiction. Things need not be, nor did they have to be as they were. What the world *de facto* is became entirely subordinated to what it could have been and what it might become. The facticity of the finite is one thing. The possibility it is open to is quite another.

Despite this radical contingency of the finite Ockham was willing to accept a willed order of things as a manifestation of God's *potentia ordinata*. It is possible for one to read and come to an understanding of that order. One could, for example, speak reasonably of cause and effect, of mutual relationships, of similarity and likeness. Hence, natural science was, indeed, possible. It is clear what great strides were made in this area, if one considers the development of natural science during the fourteenth century. Such development is often interpreted as a logical result of the restriction of human knowledge to an experienceable world and its inevitable turning away from the transcendent. Just as mysticism and pietism were two reactions, so the need to concentrate on what was available to human inquiry led quite readily to an increasingly richer understanding of the world as the most proper and most available object.

But it remained necessary to maintain that such conclusions were always more or less probable with regard to the realm of things, however necessary they were in the logical order. The *potentia Dei absoluta* was always in the background warning of other possibilities and a higher or at least unsuspected cause or causes at work. Ockham could agree with Aquinas that *intelligere sequitur esse*. But where Aquinas had distinguished between a proper object of man's understanding and an adequate object which opened up human intelligence to all of being, Ockham was unwilling to admit such a distinction. The existing singular was for ockham the intellect's proper object and its adequate object as well. The being in question here was a material human being, and the intellect of such a being had to be as limited as the being itself.

Such a world posed a direct denial of all that the neo-Platonists or the Latin Averroists stood for. There is no possibility of a necessary creation or a necessary emanation or a necessity within the world itself. Ockham's skillful reinterpretation of the doctrine of the divine ideas had removed the last vestige of such necessity from the creative act itself and from all representations of God's necessary intelligibility from any of its created manifestations. Instead of a Divine Intellect acting in accord with the intelligibility identical with itself and serving as a paradigm for all activity outside itself, there was a Divine Will—acting in accord with the principle of noncontradiction to be sure—which guaranteed both the being and the meaning of all else. What that Divine Will was like in itself was simply unknowable, and what it could or could not accomplish went far beyond its *de facto* expression in the world open to our knowledge. Ockham had his free God. The question that immediately arises is: Was the price he had to pay too high?

In general historians of philosophy, at least those who themselves were unwilling to limit philosophy to a completely empirical investigation, have judged it to be so. The difficulties which arise are by no means minor ones. For example, when theology is no longer accepted as a guide and a guarantor of natural reason but is separated from it, reason as Ockham saw it is bound to be in trouble. Or when the faith which theology investigates is itself rejected or at least left out, a great deal of certitude goes with it. One is then restricted to some sort of empirical approach to this world. What does one do with what transcends that world? And how can the transcendent be made meaningful in any way? Or how does one escape from the facticity of the finite? On the philosophical level it seems impossible to do so. For Ockham it was faith which guaranteed the truth which the finite could not. Without faith there is only one possible other way, and that is through some experience of the transcendent.

For Ockham faith had interpreted experience. But if the emphasis is placed on experience instead of faith, as it came to be in the Ockhamism which followed, then experience had to interpret faith. And since all experience is necessarily individual, whatever meaning faith has must also be restricted to the individual. Truth itself becomes whatever the individual can derive from his own personal experience. Thus everyone can become a theologian or a moralist. It had been thought that Plato had once and for all refuted Protagoras. But the position of Protagoras, that the (individual) man is the measure of all things was again to have its day, and that day has lasted long beyond the fourteenth century. Ockham would certainly have rejected the above position, but granted the conditions listed above he would have recognized it as one possible consequence.

Another difficulty surfaces with the whole notion of certitude. Ockham had never rejected certitude, even though he placed it primarily in the realm of faith and a theology operating within faith. He could afford from his perspective to recognize philosophy as highly probable and even helpful knowledge. But most philosophical conclusions which Ockham regarded as certain lay in the logical order, where certain relations were recognized as obtaining between concepts and propositions. It was quite another matter, when one had to deal with the world of existing singulars. Conclusions about that real world became certain only when and if they could be assumed and absorbed and guaranteed by faith and revelation and a theology that could fit them into that order.

The position is clearly more Augustinian than Aristotelian. And it works in Augustinianism. But once faith and revelation are removed from the system, there is little or no certitude left. This becomes even more clear when one recalls that Ockham, like Scotus, had rejected the illumination theory that had grounded and explained the possibility of certain knowledge even in the natural order for St. Augustine. Scotus had maintained that certitude could be achieved without illumination both with regard to the order of nature and the transcendent. But Ockham could not do that. Ockhamism became an Aristotelianized Augustinianism without the safeguards of either one.

If one looks only at Ockham himself, then, even if one cannot agree, there has to be a great amount of admiration for what he accomplished. Not only did he have to reject much of the work of his predecessors, but he also had to reorganize and rebuild a system of philosophy and theology to achieve the purpose he had in mind. If that purpose, as I have suggested, was to establish beyond doubt the divine freedom in both creation and in the conservation of what had been created, then from that viewpoint he was successful. But at the same time to do that he had to rewrite whole areas of epistemology, logic, and natural theology. It is in these areas, of course, where all the difficulties arise.

It is here too where his opponents have found him an easy target for rejection and criticism. That there is much to criticize is clear enough. Almost all who went before him—Augustine, Anselm, Bonaventure, Aquinas, and Scotus—would have had great difficulty with the means he used to achieve his purpose. Certainly all the persons listed above held God's freedom in creating. Bonaventure and Aquinas had vigorously criticized and attacked Latin Averroism. Neither would they have understood why the divine ideas had to be dispensed with in order to maintain that freedom. None of them sees the ideas in the mind of God as determining the Divine Will. And they were able to hold an essential necessity in creation along with its existential contingency. Ockham's universe was totally contingent, and the *potentia Dei ordinata*, "the way things generally happened," was not enough to stabilize it.

Furthermore the extent to which Ockhamism was pushed and the uses made of it in the universities did not result in a very fortunate outcome. Perhaps no philosopher or theologian has ever been very much helped by his commentators and followers. But they are bound to show up, and they tend to work out conclusions contained only implicitly in the work of the original thinker. Those conclusions themselves provide an indication of what is right or wrong with the source from which they spring. From that perspective, too, Ockham had not fared well. He has been seen as an anti-Papalist, a forerunner of Luther and the Protestant revolt, as well as a sceptic and a fideist. He has been regarded, and here unjustly, as the source of all the nominalism that has pervaded philosophy since his time.

It is highly improbable that Descartes ever read Ockham, but he certainly was aware of the conceptualism and nominalism that was present in the late medieval philosophy which he had studied at La Fleche. Against that background it is not too difficult to understand why he dreamed his dream of restoring absolute certainty to philosophy. And even then there would be the nominalistic attacks of Locke and Hume to question the validity of Descartes' attempt. For all of that it seems fair to say that Ockham was no mere nominalist but was in many ways an original and independent thinker who had his own distinct influence on both philosophy and theology. He was more than a negative critic of the great system makers of the thirteenth century and, in his endeavor to find certitude not in human reason alone but in the truth of revelation and faith, less than the sceptic he has been made out to be. Ockham may well have been convinced that he had made Christians out of the metaphysicians.

The attempts to interpret a philosopher and theologian as rich and complex as William of Ockham have been many and varied. One needs only to glance through any bibliography on Ockham to see how true this is. There has been a great interest in recent years in his logic and epistemology, but I do not think that the key to his thought lies there. Others have suggested that the main purpose in Ockham's work was to attack the Averroism rampant at the University of Paris in the thirteenth and fourteenth centuries.[1] Such an attack is clearly there in Ockham's writings. Others have concentrated on the divine omnipotence as a pivotal point in Ockham's thought.[2] That also is true. Both of the above approaches can surely be included in and reconciled with the notion of the divine freedom as Ockham's overriding concern. But both the divine omnipotence and the divine freedom have to be seen in a theological context and not just a philosophical one.

---

[1]Cf. for example, Baudry, L., "Le Tractatus de Principiis Theologiae attribué à G. D'Ockham." *Études de Philosophie Médiévale* (Paris, J. Vrin, 1936).

[2]Pernoud, M.A., "Innovation in William of Ockham's References to the 'Potentia Dei,'" *Antonianum,* vol. 45, 1970.

The philosophical probability derived from a reason no longer sure of itself beyond the realm of experience—and to a great extent within experience itself-looked for help from outside itself. That help could be given to reason along with a stability and certainty, when reason functioned in union with faith and theology. If Ockham could have read his philosophical critics, I do not think he would have been too concerned. In all probability he would have considered them as clear examples of what he had always maintained. One simply cannot expect very much of reason when it attempts to operate in isolation from a higher truth. Just as Augustine and the Augustinian tradition had always held that reason did not become less by operating within faith, so Ockham, too, never surrendered the *Credo ut intelligam.*

Finally it is important to emphasize just how dominating and essential the notion of freedom is in all of Ockham's thought. Both on the level of the infinite and the finite, freedom is at the heart of reality. We have seen in his discussion of final causality how far Ockham was willing to go to extend human freedom. Faith may well assure us that man's ultimate end is the vision of God, but no such assurance is available, if one looks at the human will from only a philosophical viewpoint. Ockham saw no way to demonstrate that it was impossible for the human will to choose ends consecutively and indefinitely. Furthermore, human freedom was such that the will could even reject the vision of God as its proper end.

It is true that God had revealed the ten commandments as a law to be followed, if man is to achieve his goal. And human reason itself can see the binding force of such commands, at least in the present order. But reason can set up other goals, and the will remains free to follow them and reject the Divine Will. Human freedom includes, if not necessarily as part of its nature, at least the capability of extending itself to ends and goals not consonant with the *de facto* order of things. Actuality is again seen as a limited expression of the possible. And possibility in a way remains a threat to this particular order of the actual. For what is possible can enter the actual at any time either as an end chosen by the free individual, or as a goal imposed from without by an omnipotent Divine Will. And this is true both in the order of being and in that of morality.

This distinction on the finite level between what is and what could be looks to or reflects something of an infinite source of actuality and possibility. The two are not, of course, really distinct in God but point to a distinction which shows up in creation. Just as God is free to create or not, so too is He free to create in this way or that. Hence the chosen created order can reveal only in a very limited way the absolute power which infinitely transcends the divine choice. Or, to say it another way, the *Potentia Dei Absoluta* is revealed only partially and inadequately in the *Potentia Dei Ordinata.*

The actuation of a limited possibility by God in no way affects or circumscribes His unlimited power. The difficulty shows up only on our side. Our knowledge of God is necessarily limited to and proceeds only as far as the way God has chosen to manifest Himself. Beyond that there is only the inaccessible light of the Absolute. Hence God still remains free to enter and function within the order He has created, and our knowledge must at least recognize this further possibility—even though such possibilities may never be realized, or at least only rarely. It is the price one pays for finitude in the face of the Infinite. Or, perhaps, better yet, it points out clearly the reason for the inadequacy of both our knowledge and our freedom in the face of Absolute Freedom.

If the God of Augustine can be properly named as the Self-Same or the Immutable, and the God of Aquinas the Pure Act of Existence, and the God of Scotus the Infinite, then for Ockham the proper name of God has to be Omnipotent Freedom, which transcends all attempts of finite intelligence to interpret it or decipher it. It is true, as we have seen, that Ockham admits a proper concept of God, but that concept, composed as it is from the finite order, says hardly anything at all of the source of that order. It is at best a substitute for that source. The Divine Actuality disappears behind the infinite variety of what is possible. However much Ockham had to change and even reject previous approaches to metaphysics and epistemology, he had at last his free God.

Selected Bibliography

Primary Sources
Ockham's Works

Guillelmi De Ockham, *Opera Philosophica et Theologica ad Fidem Codicum Manuscriptorum Edita*, Cura Instituti Franciscani, Universitatis Bonaventurae, St. Bonaventure University, (St. Bonaventue NY)

Opera Theologica,

Vol. I, *I Sent.*, Prologus and Distinction I, eds. Gedeon Gal and Stephen Brown, 1967.

Vol. II, *I Sent.*, Distinctions 2-3, eds. Gedeon Gal and Stephen Brown, 1970.

Vol. III, *I Sent.*, Distinctions 4-18, ed. Girard Etzkorn, 1977.

Vol. IV, *I Sent.*, Distinctions 19-48, eds. Girard Etzkorn and Francis Kelly, 1979.

Vol. IX, *Quodlibeta* VII, ed. Joseph Wey, 1980.

Opera Philosophica,

Vol. I, *Summa Logicae*, ed. Philotheus Boehner, 1974.

Summula in Libros Physicorum, Venice, 1506.

Secondary Sources

Abbagnano, N., *Gulielmo di Occam*, Lanciano, 1931.

Adams, Marilyn McCord. *William Ockham*. Notre Dame, IN: University of Notre Dame Press, 1987.

_____ "Was Ockham A Humean About Efficient Causality?" St. Bonaventure Press: St. Bonaventure, NY. *Franciscan Studies*, Vol. 39, pp. 5-48, 1979.

Amann, E., "Occam," *Dictionnaire Théologique Catholique*, T. 11, Col. 864-904.

Becher, H., S.J., "Gottesbegriff und Gottesbeweis bei Wilhelm von Ockham," *Scholastik* 3, 1927, pp. 369-93.

Boehner, P., O.F.M., "Notitia Intuitiva of Non-Existents according to William of Ockham," *Traditio*, 1943.

_____ "Ockham's Theory of Truth," *Franciscan Studies*, 1945, pp. 138-61.

_____ "The Centiloquium Attributed to Ockham," *Franciscan Studies*, 1941, pp. 158-72.

_____ "In Propria Causa, A Reply to Professor Pegis' 'Concerning William of Ockham'," *Franciscan Studies*, 1945, pp. 37-54.

_____ "A Recent Presentation of Ockham's Philosophy," *Franciscan Studies*, 1949, pp. 443-56.

_____ "Ockham's Theory of Signification," *Franciscan Studies*, 1946, pp. 143-70.

_____ "Ockham's Theory of Supposition and the Notion of Truth," *Franciscan Studies*, 1946, pp. 261-92.

_____ "The Realistic Conceptualism of William of Ockham," *Traditio*, 1946, pp. 307-35.

_____ "The Metaphysics of William of Ockham," *The Review of Metaphysics* I, 1948, pp. 59-86.

_____ "Zu Ockham's Beweis der Existenz Gottes," *Franziskanische Studien*, 1940, Wilhelm von Ockham, Aufsätze zu seiner Philosophie und Theologie. Dietrich Coelde Verlag. Münster, Westf.

Bréhier, E., *Histoire de la Philosophie*, T. I, Paris. Felix Alcan, 1928.

Brückmüller, F., *Die Gotteslehre Wilhelms von Ockham*. München, 1911.

Canella, G., *Il Nominalismo e Guglielmo di Occam*, Firenze, 1907.

Copleston, F., *A History of Philosophy*, V. 3, *Ockham to Suarez*, The Bellarmine Series, Burns Oates and Washbourne Ltd., London, 1953.

Day, S., O.F.M., *Intuitive Cognition*, Franciscan Institute Publications, St. Bonaventure, New York, 1947.

De Wulf, M., *Histoire de la Philosoohie Médiévale*, T. 3e, 6e edition. Louvain/Paris. 1947.

Ehrle F., *Der Sentenzenkommentar Peters von Candia*, Münster, 1925. (Franziskanische Studien, Beiheft 9).

Federhofer, F., "Die Philosophie des Wilhelm von Ockham in Rahmen seiner Zeit," *Franziskanische Studien*, 1925, pp. 273-97.

Fisscher, John Martin, "Freedom and Foreknowledge." Cornell University: Ithaca, NY. *Philosophy Review*, Vol. 92, pp. 67-79, Jan. 1983.

Geyer, B., *Die Patristische und Scholastische Philosophie* (F. Überwegs Grundriss der Geschichte der Philosophie. Bd. 2), Berlin, 1927.

Giacon, C., S.J., *Guglielmo di Occam*, Saggio historico-critico sulla formazione e la decadenza della scolastica. Pubblicazione dell'Università Cattolica del Sacro Cuore, Ser. 1, vol. xxxiv, 2 vols., Milano, 1941.

Gilson, E., *La Philosophie au Moven Age*, Payot, Paris, 1947, 3e Edition.

_____ *The Unity of Philosophical Experience*, New York, 1937.

_____ *Reason and Revelation in the Middle Ages*, New York, 1938.

Guelly, R., *Philosophie et Theologie chez Guillaume d'Occam*, Louvain - Paris, 1947.

Heynck, V., O.F.M., "Ockham Literatur 1919-1949," *Franziskanische Studien*, Wilhelm Ockham, Aufsätze zu seiner Philosophie und Theologie, 1950, Dietrich Coelde Verlag' Münster, Westf.

Hochstetter, E., *Studien zur Metaohysik und Erkenntnislehre Wilhelms von Ockham*, Berlin, 1927.

_____ "Nominalismus?," *Franziskanische Studien*, 1949, Vol. 9, N. 4.

Hudson, Anne and Wilks, Michael, eds. *From Ockham to Wyclif*. Oxford: Published for the Ecclesiastical History Society by B. Blackwell, 1987.

King, H., "From St. Thomas and the Intelligible Species to Thomism, Hume and the Sensible Species," *Dominican Studies*, 1949, pp. 93-103.

Kugler, L., *Der Begriff der Erkenntnis bei Wilhelm von Ockham*, Breslau, 1913.

Leff, Gordon. *The Dissolution of the Medieval Outlook*. New York: Harper and Row, Publishers, 1976.

_____ *William of Ockham: The metamorphosis of scholastic discourse*. Manchester: Manchester University Press, 1975.

Maier, A., "Ein neues Ockham-Manuskript," *Gregorianum*, 1947, pp. 101-33.

Manser, G., "Drei Zweifler am Kausalprinzip," *Jahrb. für Philosophie und Spec. Theologie*, 1912, pp. 405-37.

Michalski, C., "Les Courants philosophiques à Paris pendant le XlV^e siècle," *Bulletin de l'Académie Polonaise des Sciences et des Lettres*, Class d'histoire et de philosophie, 1920, Cracovie, 1922.

_____ "Le Criticisme et le Scepticisme dans la Philosophie du XIVe siecle," *Bulletin de l'Académie Polonaise*, 1925.

Moody, E. A., "Ockham, Buridan and Nicholaus of Autrecourt," *Franciscan Studies*, 1947, pp. 113-46.

_____ "Ockham and Aegidius of Rome," *Franciscan Studies*, 1949, pp. 417-42.

_____ The Logic of William of Ockham, London, 1935.

Paulus, J., "Sur le Origins du Nominalisme," *Revue de Philosophie*, 1937, pp. 313-30.

_____ *Henri de Gand*, Paris, J. Vrin, 1938.

Pegis, A., "Concerning William of Ockham," *Traditio*, 1944, pp. 465-80.

_____ "Some Recent Interpretations of Ockham," *Speculum*, 1948, pp. 452-63.

Pelzer, A., "Les 51 Articles de Guillaume Occam censurées en Avignon en 1326," *Revue d'histoire ecclésiastique*, 18, 1922, pp. 240-70.

Rivaud, A., *Histoire de la Philosophie*, T. II, *De la Scholastique à l'Époque Classique*, Presses Universitaire de France, Paris, 1950.

Schuurman, Henry Jacob, Jr. "Ockham and the Problem of God's Foreknowledge." Notre Dame, IN: University of Notre Dame, 1979. (Note: This is a PhD dissertation on microfilm.)

Seeberg, R., *Lehrbuch der Dogmengeschichte*, Bd. III, Leipzig, 1930.

Sharp, D. E., *Franciscan Philosophy at Oxford in the Thirteenth Century*, Oxford, 1930.

Sladczek, F., S.J. "Ist im Konzeptualismus Ockhams die Möglichkeit der Wissenschaften, insbesondere der Real-wissenschaften Sichergestellt?," *Scholastik*, 1929, pp. 253-55.

Tornay, S. C., "William of Ockham's Nominalism," *Philosophical Review*, 1936, pp. 245-67.

Van Leeuwen, A., O.F.M., "L'Eglise, Règle de Foi dans les Écrits de Guillaume d'Occam," *Ephemerides Theologiae Lovanienses*, 1934, T. XI, pp. 249-88.

Vasoli, C. *Guglielmo d'Occam*, La Nuova Italia, Firenze, 1953.

Vignaux, P., "Nominalisme," *Dictionnaire Théologique Catholique*, T. XI, col. 733-89.

Webering, D., O.F.M., *Theory of Demonstration according to William of Ockham*, Franciscan Institute Publications, St. Bonaventure, New York, 1953.

Weinberg, Julius Rudolf. *Ockham, Descartes, and Hume: self-knowledge, substance, and causality.* Madison: University of Wisconsin Press, 1977.

Wippel, John F. (ed.). "Ockham and Final Causality" in *Studies in Medieval Philosophy*, pp. 249-72. Washington: Catholic University American Press, 1987.

Index